SOARING
STONES

A KITE-POWERED APPROACH
TO BUILDING EGYPT'S PYRAMIDS

SOARING
STONES

MAUREEN
CLEMMONS
...
DAN
CRAY

962
Clemmons

A W.H. Sunnybrae & Co. Book
Published by Delcominy Creations, LLC
531 Main Street, Suite 231
El Segundo, CA 90245

Cover design by Jeroentenberge.com
Photos courtesy of Maureen Clemmons

A pre-publication edition of this book was commissioned by the National Geographic Society, and written in conjunction with National Geographic Expedition field tests conducted in 2002.

Soaring Stones: A Kite-Powered Approach To Building Egypt's Pyramids/ Maureen Clemmons and Dan Cray. – Revised.

The preassigned control number data is on file with the Library of Congress.

ISBN 978-0-9832830-5-8

For the first time in more than four thousand years, humanity remembered to invite the wind to be its ally in raising an obelisk...

TABLE OF CONTENTS

NOTE TO READERS

This is a collaboration between Maureen Clemmons, who innovated, funded, and field-tested the wind construction concept, and Dan Cray, who authored the book. Clemmons granted Cray exclusive access to meetings, field tests, and other research efforts, which he blended with his independent reporting. The chapters are written from Cray's perspective, except where otherwise indicated.

Both Clemmons and Cray share a sincere belief that wind power, and its possible role in constructing ancient pyramids, merits scientific consideration... and your consideration.

SOARING
STONES

The Crazy Woman

G o ahead, laugh. You've looked at the photos, read the blurb, maybe you've even watched the television documentary detailing a possible link between kites and construction of the Egyptian pyramids. The whole thing sounds ridiculous, so feel free to utter some jokes.

Just be sure to get it all out of your system before you read any further.

Believe me, I understand where you're coming from. The first time I met Maureen Johnson Clemmons, I thought she was a lunatic. After all, here's a woman with no engineering credentials whatsoever, claiming she discovered one of the techniques the ancients used to construct the Egyptian pyramids. And her premise – that the Egyptians used kites to "fly" the massive, two-ton stones? Another Los Angeles nutcase.

Actually it took six months before I agreed to speak with her, and I did that as a favor to my fiancée, a software manager who happened upon Clemmons at her workplace. I'll be honest, I dreaded it. I arranged a phone interview; her story really wasn't worth my spending an hour on the freeway.

Then I listened to what she had to say, and my assumptions began to erode.

Clemmons was level-headed, intelligent, and even self-deprecating at times. Her assertions were grounded in common sense, and her concepts relied on basic principles of aerodynamics, so there was no leap of logic or physics. Most importantly, she demonstrated an in-depth knowledge of Egyptian history and was quick to point out contrasting theories of pyramid construction—an indication she wasn't trying to hide anything. We ended up talking for an hour, then meeting face to face a few days later. Twenty years later I'm still captivated, and so are construction engineers, architects, researchers at the California Institute of Technology, and just about anyone who actually takes the time to consider the rationale behind her idea. Everybody, it seems, utters the same initial response: *you're crazy*. Then they pause, give it some thought... and agree it could work.

Of course, there's a big difference between captivated and convinced. Egyptologists devote their careers to studying the hundred-plus pyramids in Egypt, collecting firsthand evidence from on-site archeological examinations—something Clemmons has never done. Universities, governments, and a handful of private entities collectively spend millions to research every imaginable aspect of the pyramids, and you don't simply cast aside the results just because some woman from Reseda, Calif., has an interesting idea.

Egyptologists, in fact, consider the subject of pyramid construction closed. "There is no mystery," Zahi Hawass, former secretary general of Egypt's Supreme Council of Antiquities, told *Time* for a 1999 article about Clemmons. "We have very good evidence, found right at the pyramids, that tells us exactly how these monuments were put together." Among the best evidence: archeo-logical remains of levers and a sand-filled ramp, strengthened by a thick layer of clay, near the site of an unfinished pyramid. In 2000, Harvard Egyptologist Mark Lehner and a team of stonemasons, quarrymen, and la-borers successfully used the sand-ramp method to erect a massive, twenty-five-ton obelisk, confirming the tech-nique as a practical means for erecting obelisks and mov-ing large stones. Egyptologists have also found papyrus writings, friezes and other artwork of men pushing such stones.

Clemmons doesn't dispute any of this but she also knows that even today, construction techniques are rarely static. The Egyptian pyramids differ not only in size and location but in their construction plans, materi-als, and methods. Several were built using a mix of per-fectly aligned, well-engineered masonry with crude fragments of stone. Others were fashioned like an onion, using layers of horizontal strata. Some pyramids feature stones with seams for locking the blocks in place; others do not. There may also be no single, definitive solution to pyramid construction since the work occurred over the course of nearly one thousand years in different places and varying sizes. The ancient Egyptians would almost certainly have employed a variety of methods as they refined or even streamlined their techniques from experience.

More importantly, construction theories fashioned around heavy lifting have a flaw we all recognize on an instinctual level: they don't jibe with human nature. People would not physically push, pull, and hoist three-ton boulders when the technology of their era offers an easier alternative. Why would an engineer faced with the challenge of constructing the greatest monuments of his age ignore the culture's linen, one of their most abundant products? Why would they ignore their sails, one of the few technologies they had? Would they also ignore the wind, one of their civilization's primary resources? As Clemmons notes, that doesn't even make sense if you're using slaves because you're not going to have them rely on a method that will take three times as long when you could have them finish the job and move on to something else.

Hawass maintains that such arguments merely cast doubt over legitimate research and suggests Clemmons fits the profile of a pyramid-obsessed individual pursuing a preposterous construction theory. "They link together the most circumstantial pieces of 'evidence' to fit their crazy ideas," he said, "but it's not science." Clemmons, he said, is "what Egyptologists call a 'pyramidiot'—a person who ignores all sense and reason in favor of her own fantasy."

Few contest Hawass' judgment given the extensive efforts he has made to balance research and preservation with public access at some of the world's most cherished monuments. But Hawass and many of his Egyptology colleagues share years of being blunted by wild ideas, making it easy to dismiss Clemmons as another pyramidiot. Does Clemmons take the imaginative leaps of an amateur? Yes... until she finishes brainstorming, at which time she recognizes such leaps are no longer acceptable—which is exactly the way good science should be conducted. Does she claim Egyptologists' explanations for the pyramids are baseless? Not a chance. As she puts it:

This isn't about bashing on Egyptologists. What I'm saying is that sometimes it takes someone with an outside perspective to notice things that everyone in the inner circle hasn't. All I want is for these people to listen to someone who thinks differently than they do. God knows, Egyptologists get every manner of fruitcake telling them how the pyramids were built, and I suppose after too many years of it you just stop listening altogether.

Well, I'm not claiming I'm a genius, but I'm no fruitcake either. When you look at the natural resources of ancient Egypt, three things come to mind: a lot of sand, the Nile river, and a ubiquitous wind. At the same time, we're talking about a culture—ancient Egypt—that was the number one manufacturer of linen in the ancient world. We already know for a fact that the ancient Egyptians patched their linen into large sails and used them on their feluccas—ancient sailboats—to navigate the Nile. No one disputes that... which means no one disputes the fact the ancient Egyptians, in an era of extremely limited technology, understood the simple technology involved in harnessing the wind.

I've read all about the major theories of construction, but that doesn't mean they are the be-all, end-all of what it took to assemble a pyramid. Even today, there are a lot of methods to build a high-rise. Ask someone how high-rises were built in the twentieth century, and you're going to get several different answers. Egyptologists pontificate about their theories as if they were law, and maybe they can slide a few blocks together, but in the end they can't really demonstrate how a group of people managed to take millions of heavy stones, some of them weighing more than seventy tons, and not only haul them across the desert but then lift them hundreds of feet into the air. They'll talk all day long about how they think it can be done, but ask one of them to show you. That's when they go quiet.

Again, I'm not trying to bash Egyptologists—just the opposite, in fact. I'm trying to help them, to get them to open their minds without feeling insulted, or letting some weird personal pride affect their judgment. There's a whole new field of research to be opened up here... the use of wind in ancient construction. So far, nobody's touched it. They just can't seem to see it. Or maybe they just don't want to.

That doesn't change the fact that Egyptologists are experts and she is an amateur, and it certainly doesn't change the fact she is competing with a dynasty's worth of professional and amateur voices when it comes to tackling pyramid construction. But Clemmons wields some notable credentials that go well beyond her array of field tests. She brings intangibles to the table, such as an unusually strong family upbringing in science... undergraduate studies in physics... a business management EdD with an emphasis on innovation... a career teaching executives how to think and operate differently from their competition. Perhaps just as important, Clemmons also brings the can-do, never-say-die spirit of exploration reminiscent of many pioneers' biographies, coupled with a passionate ambition to show her two children that the individual, not the credential, is the key to science.

Look, I'm not an Egyptologist. I didn't expect these people to drop everything they've been working on for forty years and say, 'oh yeah, I guess we somehow missed that.' All I want these people to do is sit down and think about an approach no one else has considered. That's all I want ANYONE to do. Go ahead, laugh—hey, it's funny to think of people grabbing their kite and heading off to work in the morning. And a big ol' stone hanging from the ropes of a kite? Sure, it's an image that makes you laugh. But when you finish laughing, just stop and think about it. Sometimes crazy ideas are the road to truth, for precisely the reason they are considered crazy: because no one usually thinks about things in an alternative way.

Nearly every innovator in history has faced the same scrutiny, the same scorn. I'm not comparing myself with Ben

Franklin, or Copernicus, or any other great innovator. I'm just someone who tries to take a look at problems from a different perspective. It's what I do for a living; it's what I teach my children; it's the approach I take when I tackle my own personal issues. Sometimes looking at something from the outside can be as valuable as it is from the inside. That's not philosophy, it's common sense.

Maybe the professional Egyptologists are right: maybe Maureen Clemmons is a pyramidiot. But the more I spoke with her, the more it became clear her story is not simply about a tantalizing solution to the mystery of pyramid construction. It's about academia's steadfast refusal to consider the opinion of anyone outside of their insular circle; it's about a successful woman and her efforts to bust her way into a dialogue dictated by centuries-old theories; it's about the struggle of a middle-class, working mother to raise her children as intellectuals. Most of all, it's about the importance of approaching conundrums from a different perspective... and a bit of imagination.

Every one of us has had a "eureka moment," a time when we stumbled upon something unusual and turned

it over and over in our mind, wondering whether anyone else had given it any thought. Usually we let the idea
go, telling ourselves it's too difficult to pursue, too unusual to pan out, too silly to retain our dignity. Our heads
are packed with ambitious figments forcefully relegated
to the confines of imagination.

Maureen Clemmons doesn't let things go. She looked
at the level of engineering the Egyptians must have mastered to undertake a project as immense as the pyramids,
and decided they must have had better construction
techniques than lugging seventy-ton stones with sheer
muscle. She sought a possible solution, did some research, and found one—however unlikely. And while her
reasoning is certainly not anything approaching hard
evidence, the picture that began unfolding when she
chose to remain outside the box is fascinating. So fascinating, in fact, that it was enough to compel her—and at
least one skeptical journalist—to investigate further.

CHAPTER ONE

Foundations

With all the hours I've spent doing yard work, I thought I knew my property pretty well. That's why I was so surprised when, on a blustery February day, I discovered I had a fruit tree growing in the backyard. I'd never seen it before, and I've never seen it since. But I know it must have been there, at least on that particular afternoon, because that was the day I was hit on the head with Newton's apple.

If a frivolous, Newtonian spirit chose to pelt Clemmons, its "apple" actually came a month earlier in the form of some food for thought offered by a magazine article... an article she might not have read if not for an unusually quiet Saturday evening in January of 1997. Normally the Clemmons household served as the kind of children's repository you find in every neighborhood, that special home on the block where the rugs are always covered in footprints and the front yard is filled with every kid who lives nearby. Sometimes Clemmons would stand outside and see her own children—six-year-old Elizabeth and three-year-old Sean. Most times, however, the kids' friends and neighbors were over so the place was filled with a dozen kids. The one constant was noise—not the annoying racket of a jackhammer but the cheerful background of kids at play.

This particular Saturday had been one of those afternoons where the enthusiastic horde of kids seemed ever-present, so by the time evening rolled around and Elizabeth and Sean were in bed Clemmons noticed—she actually looked around and noticed—that her house was perfectly quiet. It was the kind of opportunity any wife/mother/career woman cherishes above all: quiet time with some good reading material. In this case she had already finished her doctoral homework, her husband, John, was off watching TV, and the kids were asleep. Thrilled, Clemmons pulled out her aunt's hand-crocheted "reading quilt" and curled up on the couch to catch up with *Reader's Digest*, *National Geographic*, and *Smithsonian*.

After about an hour of reading, her mind kept returning to a *Smithsonian* piece authored by Evan Hadingham. The article described an attempt by the public television program *Nova* to test theories of how the ancient Egyptians raised the giant obelisks that, along with the Egyptian pyramids, are icons of ancient Egyptian civilization. *Nova's* crew included stonemasons, antiquities experts, two hundred laborers, and Harvard Egyptologist Lehner, all attempting to transport and then erect two granite obelisks at the site of an ancient quarry in Aswan, some 440 miles south of Cairo. One obelisk measured only a few feet high and weighed two tons, the other forty-three feet and forty tons; both were a fraction of the 100-foot, 300-ton monoliths routinely raised by the pharaoh's workers more than three thousand years ago.

Using ramps, sand pits, levers, and "brakes" (a series of ropes wound around logs), *Nova's* team successfully raised the two-ton obelisk. But working with the forty-ton version proved much more dangerous and strained the definition of "elbow grease" to its breaking point. In the end, even with 200 men tugging at the ropes for nearly two days, they managed to lift the obelisk only two inches above a forty-degree pitch.

Clemmons absorbed the test results, fascinated that modern-day workers could not replicate a process mastered thousands of years earlier. She re-read portions of the article, looked at the photos of the researchers' Herculean efforts, then re-read the article again. Her mind kept telling her something wasn't right, and the pit of her stomach felt like someone had just insisted two-plus-two equals five. Wondering what the problem was, she ignored the text and stared at the photos, studying them, looking at the strained expressions on the faces of dozens of men as they tried to heave a chunk of stone. The images kept triggering the same nagging feeling. It wasn't just the obvious struggle, or the discomfort on the faces— though that was a big part of it. There was something else... the desert heat. These people were not only trying to use little more than sheer muscle to move an enormous stone—a bit of a stretch to begin with—but they were doing it in the desert heat. Stone amplifies the heat,

Clemmons realized, so if you're living in the middle of the Egyptian desert no one would want a construction plan that makes you feel twice as bad. That, she decided, made about as much sense as trying to push giant snowballs across Antarctica.

She looked at the photos again, at the big group of guys sweating and straining and pushing and pulling... just to move one stone a few inches. The story's author said the organizers hoped to try again but as Clemmons was reading, her inner voice was screaming at her: no, no, no! The process was way too hard—all of that pushing and sweating just to move one rock, and they hadn't even lifted it. How much more effort it would take to build an entire pyramid? No one would spend their lifetime working that way, she decided, especially without any possibility of seeing the goal achieved. As far as Clemmons was concerned, that meant there had to be an easier solution, one more compatible with human nature.

Usually when amateur scientists reach this juncture they start to tell you they've channeled unseen gods or experienced a vision after downing a few stiff drinks and therefore don't care whether other people buy into it or not. Clemmons doesn't do that. Instead, she talks about her children. She and John, determined to offset their long work hours with knowledge-enriching activities for the kids, had just spent several months in Scottish Highland dance classes and sensed a new opportunity.

Maureen, in particular, was determined to raise their kids with a thorough appreciation for science, just as her own parents had raised her. Her father, Loering, was an electrical engineer who spent twenty-five years working on nuclear power plants and made a point of teaching Maureen the value of critical thinking... and how to cobble shoes, fix the plumbing, repair the car, or put a better engine on the lawnmower. Her mother, Maral, was a homemaker who shared Loering's appreciation for independent thought and would invent "science expeditions" for Maureen, her sisters Victoria and Mara, and her brother Marc. Usually the expeditions were pretty minor: collecting rocks, feathers, or bugs. More often than not, however, they involved field trips to museums, athenaeums, or observatories.

Maureen's upbringing, and her subsequent approach to raising children, went hand in hand with the way her husband John was raised. His parents, Eileen and Jack

Clemmons, made a similar effort to underscore the value of education—not necessarily the kind of education taught in school, but an admiration for the actual process of learning. Growing up, Eileen and Jack were constantly buying books and encouraging John to use them as a starting point for independent thought. Jack, especially, hammered home the idea John should never accept what he read without thinking things through and, when possible, physically ascertaining that truth—much the same message that Maral and Loering Johnson had given Maureen.

Two decades later, she and John wanted Elizabeth and Sean to have the combined philosophies of extensive reading mixed with family science expeditions. When Elizabeth (and later Sean) turned four, Maureen began organizing backyard science projects that they and Muhammad Khan, a close friend and neighbor who was the same age, could work on together. They spent their weekends learning how to make soap, candles, ceramics, and wood carvings. They built primitive boats out of fur, or rawhide, or wood, then floated them in the bathtub. They made medicine from nasturtiums, marigolds, and other garden plants. They tried fishing and crabbing, and learned what was safe to eat if they were lost in the woods. Craft times were equally instructional: they added beads to clothing, and used needles attached to magnets or lodestones to point their way north. They learned to work with tools in the garage, or use rocks to create campfires. Since Maureen taught the kids' Sunday school class, she saw to it that Elizabeth and Sean learned Christian history and culture, comparative religion, and the fundamentals of Greek and Latin.

The kids, of course, wanted excitement with their lessons, so Maureen mixed in a dose of weapons training: Elizabeth, Sean and Muhammad had to make their own toy bows and arrows using tomato sticks, feathers, wire, and sinew. Later they tried sword fighting, crafting their own swords from wood and setting the stage for Loering, a fencer, to mimic the way Viking fathers taught their sons: by practicing swordplay on sand. Before long the Clemmons' neighbors—amazed to discover Elizabeth, Sean and Muhammad knew so many skills—were asking to have their kids join the fun. That led to the amusing summer day when Maureen, tired of her children leaving their dirty clothes all over the house, decided to give them an appreciation for clean clothes by having them and a row of their friends use rocks and washbasins to wash their clothes in the front yard while neighbors giggled.

The Egyptologists' attempts to raise the forty-ton obelisk triggered Clemmons's creative juices in much the same fashion. She started wondering how she could launch the kids into a hands-on science project involving the mystery of the pyramids. Building miniature pyramids out of sugar cubes was one option, but that was too easy—the kids wouldn't get the physical feel of moving rock. Of course, she couldn't have small children working with life-sized pyramid stones, either. That would be too dangerous—and where would she find the stones, anyway? The grand alternative, taking the kids on a field trip to Egypt, was not an option; as a two-income family the couple covered their expenses and managed to put some money in the bank, but their most elaborate family vacation was a trip to North Dakota. Besides, Clemmons figured, visiting exotic locales was not the point of the family projects. The goal was to come up with something constructive for the gang to work on, together, for a few hours over the weekend.

When Clemmons finally put the magazine away and went to sleep, her subconscious continued working on the challenge. She thought about it again the next day, over breakfast, and later that afternoon when the family was practicing their highland dances. It was the type of minor dilemma she enjoyed: the need to come up with an innovative science project that didn't re-tread over old ideas. Best of all, it actually played to Clemmons's professional and academic strengths. As vice president of Sebastian International, a hair-care products company, her job focus was to induce "change management"—a buzzword that boils down to increasing productivity by altering the way executives perceive their marketplace. [Clemmons later utilized the same philosophy as CEO of her own hair-care company, and currently as a business consultant specializing in innovative thinking.] Her doctoral work at Pepperdine University, where she held an MBA in management, focused on the concept of innovation. She even had an academic background in science; in her days as an undergraduate student at California State University, Northridge, she majored in physics before shifting to business. Together, Clemmons's professional and academic skills, along with her upbringing, were geared towards melding facts with innovative thinking—a good formula for a would-be trailblazer.

The pyramid dilemma not only fell in line with her routine thought processes, it raised its head at her daily since Sebastian Inc. was headquartered in a glass-sided, pyramid-shaped building. Clemmons decided the key to coming up with a suitable science project was to take an existing theory and see if she and the kids could work it through on their own—just like the *Nova* team, only on a much smaller scale... and a much smaller budget. Of course, that meant she needed a hypothesis, some basis for forming an experiment that she and the kids could handle. So she did the very thing her innovation training taught her to do: forced herself to stop using any conventional thinking when mulling ancient Egyptian construction.

It's not as easy as it sounds. For at least a month, Clemmons couldn't do it. Every idea she came up with involved some sort of pushing or pulling, so she knew she still needed to shut down those impulses—to consciously force herself to block out any pushing and pulling methods and see what was left. Still, every day she found her mind pushing and pulling those stone blocks all over again.

She mentioned her mental musings to John, who recognized she was onto her latest scientific scent and would not let up until she figured out a way for them to have some fun with it. Maureen Clemmons is not unlike one of the 15-year-old college graduates you see on the news: educated, but with an ingratiating element of unpredictability. She is equally at ease discussing history, scientific postulates, obscure trivia, and passages from the Bible as she is debating the nuances of her family's most recent tag football game. But just when you think she is all quotes, numbers and anecdotes, she'll contort her face and voice to imitate one of her friends, or throw in verbal expressions along the lines of, "well, duh!" At important business meetings, Clemmons is as likely to request a group photo—"this is so fun, I can't believe I'm actually doing this" is her common refrain—as she is to hammer forth the point of the meeting. As a result, she has an uncanny knack for putting even the most uptight acquaintances at ease.

Clemmons also personifies what people in chichi regions of Los Angeles have long stereotyped as a typical

San Fernando Valley resident: hard-working and am-
bivalent about social status. She wears very little makeup,
usually dresses in T-shirts, and often keeps her hair tied
back in a simple, maintenance-free braid. Her voice is
commanding and occasionally coarse, but almost always
offset with a gregarious laugh. That aura, of a real person
living amid a sea of pretense, has disarmed critics ever
since she moved to Los Angeles from her native Connecticut in the 1970s.

Clemmons knew that simply coming up with some
half-baked theory wasn't enough. After years of working
on family science projects, she understood that whatever
she came up with had to be something plausible, something so well thought-out that even her father and his
engineer's mind would sit back and debate whether it
could work. That meant tossing out the reams of implau-
sible concepts—no pyramid-building UFOs, no cults
erecting the monuments through witchcraft, no sign-
posts placed by God. No, Clemmons decided, this wasn't
about inventing the impossible, it was about reasoning
through the evidence from a different perspective and
determining what was possible.

Clemmons already had a pretty good handle on that evidence from her extensive reading and a personal interest in archeology. Car rides and Thanksgiving dinner conversations often turned to the latest findings in the Valley of Kings. She knew that the ancient Egyptians didn't have domesticated horses and had limited resources, but were versed in mathematics—not as a subject unto itself, but as applied to practical engineering. As far as Clemmons was concerned, that meant they would likely combine math with one of their few resources when it came time to solve engineering problems.

A day or so after Clemmons reached that point in her reasoning, the Santa Ana winds started blowing through Reseda. The Santa Anas, named for their point of origin in California's Santa Ana River valley, blow from the desert towards the sea at speeds exceeding twenty-five knots until high pressure funnels the air through the passes and canyons northeast of Los Angeles. At that point they accelerate to speeds of thirty-five knots, whipping through the L.A. Basin with gusts up to sixty knots. The Santa Anas usually begin in October, but often continue into winter... which is exactly what happened on the February day when Clemmons's subconscious was still pondering the pyramid issue. She went outside to do some yard work, expecting to be pushed around by the breeze, and felt a blast of inspiration instead. As leaves flew around her and strong gusts nudged her body forward, an idea popped into her mind.

"The Egyptians used the wind," she said to herself.

She mulled it, playing with the concept, turning it over, tasting a new food. She thought about the "Thousand Winds of Egypt." She remembered historical accounts of the Vikings' attempt to enter Constantinople from the desert by raising their sails, putting their longships on rollers, and "sailing" across the sands. She recalled references to "gods" raising monuments in Egyptian literature—and gods, by most ancient definitions, tend to be invisible, powerful, and live in the sky. Then she thought of images she had seen on TV of trees uprooted in strong winds.

"The Egyptians used the wind," she repeated. "They were sailors, just like the Vikings."

It never occurred to her that all she had done was take three unrelated pieces of trivia and mash them together as part of a unified theory. It was pulp archaeology: she had solved a mystery by fingering a suspect that loosely fit all of the clues. In this conundrum, however, there was no smoking gun and no improbable confession as soon as she pointed her finger.

What she had were some legitimate historical anecdotes. While Middle Eastern climate has changed over the course of five thousand years, the Thousand Winds of Egypt are generally thought to be the stronger predecessors to today's "khamsin" winds that sweep across the country's deserts at speeds of 30 miles per hour every March through June. There seems little question that the Giza plateau was the site of a consistent source of wind. As for the Vikings sailing their ships over land, author Gwyn Jones writes in *A History of the Vikings* that 200 vessels carrying 80,000 men used log rollers and the wind to sail across the desert and attack Constantinople in 907 AD. Even though the attack failed, the event suggests people of the era were very familiar with the concept of using sails to harness the wind, even on dry land. Clemmons's reference to the "gods" raising monuments is less reliable—written literature supporting the claim refers to efforts to raise stelae (obelisks) in ancient Ethiopia. It seems likely that most ancient cultures viewed gods as invisible, powerful entities that live in the sky, just as

Clemmons suggests. That certainly doesn't mean the Egyptians were correlating gods to wind... but as she points out, it doesn't mean they weren't, either.

Still, she had no hard evidence... and as Clemmons's glow faded, she began to realize exactly that. Proving her idea meant determining exactly how the Egyptians harnessed the wind... and demonstrating the answer, she figured, would form the basis for the family's next backyard science project. Again she considered the Vikings and their sails, wondering whether the Egyptians might have assembled large kites from sailcloth and then used them to lift the three-ton pyramid stones into place. The mental image was too much, and Clemmons laughed to herself after thinking about it. Then she thought about it again, and it didn't seem so funny since wind produces tremendous amounts of force—enough to topple houses and blow big-rig trucks across the freeway. Comparing that force to the miniscule amount produced by manual labor, she realized, was even more amusing than the idea of kites lifting blocks.

"Think about it: if you tied a rope around an oak tree, how many men would it take to pull it out of the ground?" she told John that night. "Dozens, possibly hundreds. But the wind outside my house can pull up a tree at any time. By the same standard, how many people would you need to produce enough force to push a house onto its side—not using tools, but with sheer strength? There's no comparison. The wind carries an amazing amount of energy, so if you could harness that energy and put it to work for you, a three-ton pyramid stone wouldn't seem like much of a problem at all. And the truth is, you can harness that energy. All you need is a kite and some strong line. You'd attach two or three kites to one of the pyramid stones and let the wind lift it into place for you."

John thought about it and agreed it made sense. "The truth is," he said, "as long as someone's not coming into it with some other agenda, it's a very palatable idea." But he also pointed out there was no archaeological evidence of the ancients using such a method. That's when Maureen realized that if the ancients used sails or kites it might also explain why there isn't much physical evidence of their construction tools and techniques.

"What is there to find?" she said. "Kite frames, rope, and sails. The kite frames were so lightweight they would never have survived four thousand years. The rope and sails were probably recycled for other projects and eventually eroded from time. Other than that there's just wind… and that's still there, whipping by the pyramids just as it always has."

She decided the concept was sensible enough to put it to its first test: an inquisitive phone call to her father, the retired engineer. Loering Johnson didn't laugh when she told him the Egyptians built their pyramids using wind, he just dryly delivered, "Of course they did—how else would they have done it?" Then he approached the matter like most disciples of physics: with mathematics. To a physicist, the rise of the sun, the rush of the tides, the glow of an aurora, and the shudder of an earthquake are all explained by scribbling a few equations on a notepad. So Johnson did just that: he scratched notes onto a pad by the phone, working over the necessary figures: the weight of the stones, the speed of the wind in Giza, the amount of surface area necessary to lift an object of the size in question. It only took him a few minutes to come to the preliminary conclusion that the physics and math behind her idea were sound. "There are still some details that need filling in," Johnson said, "but in the end the idea may give us a better understanding of what may have happened in Egypt."

And there it was: the family science project she had been looking for. Her father said they needed to fill in details. That meant they needed to conduct experiments. The kids could help with the experiments, and document the results.

In the month that followed, Clemmons began formulating the project. She went to the store and spent more than $200 on reference books, cleaning out the store's Egyptology section in her zeal to gather information. She visited the library and began searching through reams of research papers, historical data, and engineering texts to explore the possibility of using wind as an engineering tool. At this stage, her theory was still merely a gut feeling... but it was about to become much more.

CHAPTER TWO

The Johnson Experiments

The first time I truly noticed the usefulness of wind, there were timbers creaking beneath my feet, sails unfurled above my head, and beautiful blue waters splashing gently to either side. I was aboard the Dragon Ship, a boat I had helped build along with my brother and sisters in 1989. Not just any boat, mind you. No, my family couldn't just do something easy like build a routine boat. Instead, my brother and I spent weeks researching and then constructing an eighteen-foot Viking knarr, using whatever materials we could find. Our father is full-blooded Norse, so we didn't just

want to replicate a Viking journey, we wanted to be Vikings —
at least for a day.

To say Clemmons and her three siblings have a history of biting off more than they can chew is not only an
understatement, it's a disservice to their adventuresome
spirit. Prior to the Egyptian kite endeavor, the home-
made Viking knarr (a Norse merchant ship) was the family's crowning achievement when it came to extravagant
group projects. At the time Clemmons was unmarried,
attending California State University, Northridge, and
game to try just about any unusual weekend project that
would make for a great story. In the case of the Viking
knarr the lure was twice as tempting, since the Johnsons
had traced their ancestry back to 230 A.D. (another family project) and knew their entire lineage included a
hearty dose of Norwegian blood. To this day Clemmons
lovingly calls her family "a horde of Vikings," so the
thought of crafting one of their ships was particularly
appealing.

Even though the four Johnson kids had moved out of
their parents' Connecticut home and were living on their
own in Los Angeles, the occasional weekend projects

were still a part of their lives in the form of an unspoken expectation that they would help each other out whenever one of them decided to try something new. As a result, Victoria, Maureen, Marc, and Mara Johnson found themselves collaborating on each other's every whim, even after they'd moved out of the same house. No matter the idea, the time frame, or even the amount of money required to make something happen, no one thought twice about it—after all, if they couldn't afford the necessary materials from the store, they knew they could simply re-engineer something else to do the job as their father had taught them. It was no big deal, just the latest family project.

Which is why, when Marc suggested they try their hand at re-creating a life-sized Viking knarr, there was no doubt in Maureen's mind that they could research the schematics from the library, get together on weekends, gather up lumber and sailcloth, solicit some labor from enthusiastic friends, and spend a couple of months crafting and assembling the boat. They sewed the redwood planks together with fishing line, used tar to seal the joints, a tarp for a sail, and fashioned some oars.

About a month later, their 18-foot, scaled-down version of an authentic knarr was finished. Marc and Maureen had built a large, wooden dragon head and attached it to the bow, while Mara painted a series of shields along each side of the boat and a hand-crafted flag depicting a fire-breathing dragon. In the spirit of the fact they were brash, young adults, they hoisted a sail that proclaimed, "Don't F-ck With Me." They coated it with water sealant, loaded it onto a boat trailer they had specifically bought for the ship, and christened it The Valkarie. In casual conversation, however, it was always simply The Dragon Ship.

The next morning, they hauled it to a recreational lake in Los Angeles' foothills, pushed the knarr into the lake, jumped onto the deck, and raised the home-sewn sail. For about thirty glorious seconds the Johnsons and their friends were Vikings, hooting and hollering, vowing to conquer the region.

Then the ship sank.

A week later, the Dragon Ship was firewood. Even though the effort was a disaster—one friend ended up going to the hospital with a cut foot—the group decided to try again. After more research, consultations with boating experts, and a massive reconstruction job, the Dragon Ship was reborn. The Johnsons pushed it into the water and hopped onto the deck. After ten minutes the ship was still afloat, so Marc unfurled the handmade sail as Maureen bailed water from the deck. The knarr inched forward, and a crowd on shore cheered. Before long the Dragon Ship was in the middle of the lake, its passengers whooping it up and proclaiming their mock-plans to raid the ships of any Celts who strayed too close. The Dragon Ship never sailed again, but for one day the Johnsons were Vikings, celebrating another family project that worked.

Two decades later, Clemmons found herself hoping her young children could experience a similar collaborative triumph, in this case by experimenting to see whether something as simple as a kite could lift a heavy stone. Before she could start planning the experiment, however, she wanted to know whether her kite idea was historically feasible. The gaping flaw in her theory screamed at her subconscious: there is no evidence that the ancient Egyptians used kites. Archeologists have never found the remains of a kite frame, never translated a mention of kites in the hieroglyphs, and have yet to see a kite depicted in Egyptian artwork. If there was no chance the ancients used kites, Clemmons figured, why bother having the children conduct the experiment?

For several weeks, Clemmons pored through Egyptology books, analyzing published results of archeological digs at the pyramids. She stared at images of the uncovered treasures, sometimes devoting half-an-hour to a single photograph. She taught herself the basics of hieroglyph translation, then reviewed the legends she already knew about the Egyptian gods and the fundamentals of Egyptian society.

The initial challenge was the most basic: determining whether the ancient Egyptians had the materials necessary for making kites. With regard to the fabric, the answer seemed encouraging. Clemmons found books indicating that the ancient Egyptian mariners typically sewed oblong blocks of linen into sails, then reinforced them with leather patches and secured them using hemp or flax rope. She also learned that the Pharaohs controlled the ancient world's textile industry, and thus, the flax and linen that went into sailcloth. Based on that, Clemmons figured the Egyptians had plenty of resources for sowing, harvesting, and weaving flax into linen and sailcloth.

Identifying a source for the wood necessary to construct kite frames posed more of a problem since wood was scarce in ancient Egypt, but the Egyptians did have access to Lebanese cedar through trading expeditions and many Egyptologists suggest the cedar was used to make log rollers. Clemmons figured the cedar might just as easily have been used for kite frames. In addition, cedar is lightweight, strong, and easily split into lengths—perfect for building light, flexible, durable frames.

But Clemmons still had a problem, and a major one: other than their use of small sails to navigate the Nile, there is no evidence that the ancient Egyptians used kites or otherwise harnessed the wind. Or... is there? Clemmons wondered whether this was another case of relying too much on her modern perspective. She took a few days away from her research, to refresh her mind. She knew there was no indication of kites or sails in the research... at least, not stated as such. But she wondered whether this might be a case, to borrow a hackneyed phrase, of a spade not being called a spade. After all, if you're looking for a cow in a steak house, you might not find one. There's no mention of a cow on the menu; there's generally no picture of a cow on the wall; there's certainly nothing resembling a cow in the building. If you stumbled upon the vacant remains of a steak house after years of abandonment, there might not be any means of associating a cow with the house. Yet the truth is, the cow is all-important to the operation of a steak house.

She decided to take the same approach to the pyramids that she took with the Viking ship: the goal was not to study the Egyptians, it was to be an Egyptian—to think like someone living in the year 3000 BC, in a desert city, with a shorter average life span, no advanced tools, and faced with the prospect of having to construct a monument the size of a mountain. The wind was not an element, it was the hand of a god. A kite would not have been a kite, it would have been a man-made bird. And, she figured, using man-made birds for construction would have been such a spectacular, vivid sight that there would be numerous images of them reflected in Egyptian art.

She studied images of the goddess Isis, who is associated with wind. In Egyptian theology, Isis retrieved the scattered remains of her dead husband's body and then turned herself into a hawk called a "kite" so the spirit of her late husband could impregnate her. The "kite" is a bird with a very large wingspan, and the modern word "kite" derives from the bird of the same name. Clemmons found a museum replica of Isis and noticed a set of wings attached to the goddess' outstretched arms.

"If you're living in an ancient culture, how do you represent power that is invisible like wind?" she asked herself. "Or maybe the better question is, how better to represent it... than with wings?"

She returned to her reference materials and discovered that nearly every Isis image not only had wings, but that the wings are not represented in the flattened position that a bird holds its wings while flying. Instead, Isis' wings are always cocked forward, simulating the curvature of an airline wing. In other words, they are represented by a shape that forms vertical lift. Birds rarely fly with their wings held in such a position.

Clemmons was stunned. She looked at the hieroglyphs and noticed outstretched wing depictions everywhere, especially at the top-center of monuments, most with the same, odd curvature. In engineering terms, the wings have a large aspect ratio—meaning the wingspan is so dramatically extended that the wings are designed to fly straight up, at a ninety-degree angle to Earth. She wondered: could such images represent the force that raised the monuments? She checked her books and came across a photo of a building frieze on display at the Cairo Museum. The frieze depicts a wing pattern in bas relief, but the pattern does not resemble the shape of any living bird. A series of thin, vertical objects are depicted hanging from the pattern, with several men standing below—kite lines stretching down to the people, perhaps?

Recurring images of straight-winged birds with their feet spread apart also fascinated her. "It sure doesn't look like any bird I've ever seen," she thought. She tried to pull back, to picture things as if she was actually there, with the bird. No, not with the bird, she realized, but on the ground, looking at the bird soaring above... and it occurred to her that the image might depict how a kite appears from the ground: a large, narrow sail leading to a pair of legs spread apart for stability.

"Oh my god, it's been right there all along," Clemmons told John that night. "We've been looking for the answer for all these years and the Egyptians had it right there, in front of us, the whole time. We're not looking at birds on the buildings, or symbols of the sun. We're looking at some kind of kite!"

Maybe... or maybe not. Where Clemmons saw kite lines hanging from wings, others see a sculptor's random squiggles. Where she saw a sail leading to legs spread apart for stability, one could just as easily see an Egyptian Rorschach test with dozens of alternative patterns. All of which assumes the artwork doesn't depict what it appears to be in the first place: bird wings.

Clemmons recognized the leaps, so she kept investigating and noticed many of the pharaohs and winged gods were holding an ankh—an Egyptian hieroglyph which looks similar to a cross but has a large loop above the crosspiece rather than a vertical bar. According to Hieroglyphics: The Writings of Ancient Egypt by Maria Carmela Betro, the hieroglyphs generally associate the ankh with "the breath of life." In Fascinating Hieroglyphs by Christian Jacq, the ankh symbol is also used to spell the ancient Egyptian word for "block of stone." As Clemmons looked over various renderings of the ankh in ancient Egyptian art, she noticed many of them had something in common: the appearance of rope or twine around the crosspiece of the symbol. She also noticed repeated depictions of birds with outstretched wings and ankhs attached to their feet. Clemmons started wondering why the birds were always holding the ankhs. Why wasn't the emblem on their wings, or in the sky, or anywhere else? Why always in the bird's claws? There were no immediate answers.

Intrigued, she wrote her findings, suppositions, and preliminary conclusions into the form of a research paper, and on April 9, 1997, she presented the first draft of her eight-page, self-crafted study to family and friends.

They laughed. Then they cracked jokes. One person told Clemmons they were going to put an addition on their home using kites; another wanted to know what the OSHA costs of "flying stones" would be. Then everyone stopped laughing, started asking questions, and stuck Clemmons's answers on their mental scales. In a fifteen-minute span, the joke turned into a serious discussion about how using the wind for engineering applications might be feasible.

In the aftermath, Clemmons had plenty of encouragement but she also realized that mathematical equations and curious artwork would never be enough to make people believe kites could lift heavy objects. She needed a field test to demonstrate the idea, and not just a test designed exclusively for the kiddies. No, she decided, she needed a real experiment, using kites to lift something heavy... something that would make people see her concept rather than just read about it. This was no longer just for the kids. This was going to be another full-on Johnson Experiment, a project so ambitious she was going to need her friends, her parents, her siblings, her work colleagues, and anyone who cared to lend a hand.

Along with John's help and the usual assistance from her brother and sisters, Clemmons rounded up the aid of John's family and several friends. She had no restrictions: kids were as welcome as adults since flying kites for a science experiment was a very feasible project, even for young children. Everyone agreed to help with the planning, but more importantly they pledged to help when it came time for the actual field tests—a date she couldn't set in advance since it would depend entirely upon wind conditions. By this time it was nearing summer of 1997— a time of year when there isn't much wind in the Los Angeles area. In late fall, the Santa Anas would return. That meant she had roughly half a year to gather up the necessary materials. In the meantime she also needed to generate publicity about the theory, as a means of guaranteeing additional public interest when she actually demonstrated the concept.

She drove to a toy store and purchased four ordinary, plastic children's kites. Easy on the pocketbook, and easy on the kids. She also invested in a ten-dollar weather kit to monitor temperature and wind speed during field experiments, and several types of twine, tarps, and leather gloves from a hardware store. If the small, plastic kites couldn't lift anything, she figured, the tarps might.

Then came the hard part, at least from a budgetary perspective: Clemmons went to the local Army/Navy store and bought two used army parachutes for $100 apiece. The chutes were large—three-foot by four-foot—and the ropes had been cut off, but Clemmons didn't care; she needed something she could fashion into parafoil-style kites, brand new parachutes cost too much money, and her financial investment in the project was far from finished.

Economics aside, the biggest problem was determining what to have the kites lift. Ideally, the best way to demonstrate her idea would be to use stones identical in size, weight, and composition to the stones used in the actual pyramids. But as Clemmons joked with friends, she didn't own a forklift. Attaching the kite lines to large rocks also didn't seem feasible; aside from the issue of how to secure them properly, she wanted to avoid any chance of the children or the other volunteers being hurt during the experiment. The best approach, she figured, was to mimic rocket pioneer Robert Goddard, who started out with hand-held rockets before designing the kind that could reach the moon.

Clemmons knew that the ancient Egyptians had raised dozens of massive obelisks, such as the 323-ton, 100-foot high specimen still standing near the outskirts of Luxor, and figured what worked for pyramid stones would also have worked to hoist an obelisk off the ground and stand it upright. On a more practical level, she figured an obelisk would be easy to obtain since scaled-down versions of the originals are sometimes used for municipal décor and garden props.

Not so, she discovered. For seven weeks, Clemmons and a friend from work contacted statuary stores, mortuaries, furniture shops, and any business they thought might have information on where to purchase an obelisk.

Every time, it was a dead end. Finally she wandered into a garden store and stumbled across a concrete obelisk that was just under five feet tall. It wasn't ideal—Clemmons preferred something taller, in granite. But granite obelisks of the same size had to be special-ordered, and cost about $5,000 each. Clemmons decided the concrete version would do just fine. Two hundred fifty dollars later, it was hers... and with the help of a borrowed furniture dolly, she moved it into Mara's garage.

Since Clemmons wanted to make sure people had fun with the experiment, she bought pith helmets for herself, the kids, and her friends to wear at the field test. She also bought expedition clothes for Sean and Elizabeth, and dressed herself in beige khakis and a multi-pocketed vest that made her look like an amateur Jane Goodall. Determined to let her adult friends in on the fun, she ordered four cases of Pyramid Apricot Ale, an alcohol with bottles sporting pyramid images on their labels.

After several weeks scouting locations where she could conduct the field tests, Clemmons settled on Wilbur-Tampa Park, an obscure recreational area conveniently located just up the street from Mara's home, near the rim of the San Fernando Valley. Clemmons sent word to her family and friends, letting them know they were now on call to show up at the park, with little warning, as soon as windy conditions were forecast. In the meantime, Clemmons began taking Elizabeth and Sean to the park so they could practice working with kites attached to toy obelisks, and checking the wind patterns. They soon learned they needed to control the direction of the lift in order for the obelisk to stand upright.

That fall, the incidental expenses started to kick in—carabiners to secure the kite ropes to the obelisk, three delta wing kites from a specialty kite shop, another 200 feet of kite line, a videographer, tapes, a professional journal to record the experiment results… the list seemed endless. As late November rolled around, the normally reliable Santa Anas had yet to whip up and Clemmons was getting anxious.

Finally, on the evening of December 9, 1997, she checked an Internet weather site and discovered that 25 mph winds were expected from the northeast the following morning. Clemmons called her family and friends, then contacted the local news media, figuring the experiment might generate some wind/engineering dialogue among Egyptologists. Finally she kissed John and the kids good night and talked herself into thinking she was going to get a good night's sleep. The latest Johnson family science project was finally getting underway, and Maureen had little doubt that by the time it was finished the Viking ship was going to look like small potatoes.

CHAPTER THREE

Shades Of Ben Franklin

The sun took its time rising on Sunday, December 10, 1997. I can tell you that firsthand, because by the time daylight broke I was already perched atop a bluff in Wilbur-Tampa park, praying for wind. The Weather Service had issued a wind advisory, which is why I had loaded my Mitsubishi SUV with three varieties of kites and dollied the four-hundred-pound obelisk up the road from Mara's place sometime after 5 a.m. By 6:15, I was in the park, using my cell phone to call out the troops. I was calling pretty early, but no one cared because they had all committed to be ready when the day finally came, and this was it. Besides, as one of them put *it, who wouldn't want to be there for the most significant kite fly since Ben Franklin's?*

Clemmons opened the lift door on the SUV and felt butterflies in her stomach as she spotted the kites, the circus colors of their nylon exteriors folded neatly into squares. She removed one of them and ran her hands across the top, looking at it the way a NASCAR driver admires his coupe. By chance it was one of her two parafoils, a type of kite similar to the parabola-shaped chutes used by professional skydivers... and the kite she figured offered the best chance for lifting the hefty obelisk. She felt the coarseness of the nylon and the ripples in the folds. It was just backyard science, she told herself. Honest science, but backyard science nonetheless, a chance to play around and see whether her idea held any merit. Nothing more.

Yeah, she thought. Sure.

She spent the better part of an hour setting up, knowing John would bring Elizabeth and Sean a little while later. Hauling the kites, folding chairs, and other gear into the field wasn't easy; the park was located at the crest of a hill, several yards above the closest parking area, meaning everything had to be taken up an incline and across a field to reach the point with the best wind exposure. Since Clemmons arrived so early she began the process on her own. She assembled a collapsible table, went back to the car for more gear, then returned to the park to find a stranger was walking off with the table. Clemmons got the table back, but couldn't help but think the day had gotten off to an inauspicious start.

Things improved when friends arrived and helped Clemmons finish setting everything up. Soon Mara and her husband Fred showed up with their kids and a big pot of coffee, so the place began to seem much more friendly—cold and windy, but friendly. Sunrise alleviated some of the suffering, reworking shadowy figures into bushes and trees lining a beautiful park. The winds had already blown the smog out of the L.A. Basin, leaving a clear view of the hills bracketing the San Fernando Valley. By 8:30 everyone Clemmons expected had arrived, most wearing the pith helmets she had purchased. Clemmons was dressed in one as well, along with the khaki, pocketed vest and matching pants that she considered her "expedition wardrobe."

From a distance, the group looked more like picnickers than would-be scientists. Elizabeth and Sean were playing with their plastic kites on the grass, joined by some of the other kids. Friends from Clemmons's dance classes looked over the gear. Jack and Eileen Clemmons chatted with Phillip Johnson, Maureen's Pepperdine classmate, while neighbor Tom Coyle discussed the kite theory over coffee. Several other neighbors and friends commented on the force of the wind, and the fact Clemmons had managed to get so many people to help out. One man was a stranger from the community who had heard about Clemmons plan and was so fascinated by the theory he volunteered to help.

The news media arrived a short while later. Reporters from NBC and the Los Angeles *Daily News* chatted with everyone, piqued by the old-fashioned charm of a grassroots attempt at science. As cameramen and sound technicians checked backgrounds and interference, Clemmons used the time to check the wind. The gauge indicated a steady 20 mph breeze, with gusts up to 40 mph. Her prayers had been answered... but perhaps answered too well. The 40 mph gusts made it difficult to walk, much less try to fly a kite loaded with heavy objects. She decided to let the kids use their plastic kites with the miniature obelisks, then move them out of the area when she started working with the larger items; the gusts meant there was too much risk that the kids could get hurt. Even the adults were going to need some time flying the kites, to get a feel for how they would maneuver in unpredictable winds.

She brought out the pile of folded kites and removed two triangular delta wings, the nylon equivalent of the kind sold in toy stores. The rainbow-colored kites rippled and bobbed in her hands as the wind rose and fell, so Clemmons and her friends quickly hooked up the 200-lb. nylon kite line and let the deltas fly. They shot into the air simultaneously as everyone cheered and took turns at the control lines. "We can't keep the kites on a short leash because the winds are in the upper regions of the sky—and are they ever," Coyle told the group. "The park's at the downside of a hill, and the winds are coming off the top of the hill and then going back up into the atmosphere, so the further down you get the higher you have to lift the kites to get good air. Once we get the kites above forty feet, the winds are ferocious. But there's nothing in between—at thirty feet there's dead air, and at forty feet it's a veritable hurricane."

Flying the deltas was like holding a rope tied to the leg of a fluttering parakeet. The kites tugged and veered, flying up and down at wide angles with every gust. They were fun and exciting, because the controllers had to be ready to compensate for continual, unpredictable movement. But that also proved the reason they seemed an unlikely design for anyone hoping to lift heavy objects. There was too much movement, and too little means of control. Complicating matters, the kites actually bent backwards in the strong gusts, diluting their pull. Delta wing kites, Clemmons decided, were for recreational use only.

The group set the delta wings aside for the kids to have fun with and moved on to a box kite. The turquoise, rectangular kite didn't make the rippling noises of its smaller brethren, but proved more difficult to launch because the wind gusts caused its awkward shape to wobble—a problem when it was still close to the ground. After a couple of tries, the group decided to launch the kite the old fashioned way—by holding the kite string and running into the wind. The time-honored method worked; as the box kite increased altitude and unspooled more line, it proved smooth to fly and easier to control than the deltas. As she held the control line, however, Clemmons had the nagging sense that the box kite design didn't produce the necessary amount of lift to hoist something as heavy as a pyramid stone. The kite's relative lack of surface area also meant it was given to steep, vertical dips whenever the wind diminished—a dangerous characteristic, Clemmons decided, if you're in the midst of lifting a heavy stone. Box kites weren't the solution.

That left her with the parafoil... or more correctly, the parafoil left with her. The three foot by four-foot kite shot across the park as soon as Clemmons unfurled it, the wind snapping it open with a loud pop that revealed a vibrant mix of blue, yellow, orange, and green nylon. The parafoil tugged Clemmons forward as she struggled to regain her balance, digging her heels into the grass. At first everyone laughed, until John—who is six-foot-six and weighs about 240 pounds—tried it for himself and discovered he too could barely hold the kite. "The pull's incredible," John said. "That sail could take three people and move us forward like it wasn't even being held."

Worse, the tug was so strong that the kite line cut his hands, then later sliced through the palms of a pair of leather work gloves. Clemmons tried assigning two people to each kite, but the wind was so wild the kites were either down on the ground or snapping strings.

They soon found it took three people to maintain control over the parafoil, one for each control line and another for the primary line. Once they got a feel for the kite's actions they were able to angle it upwards, lofting it four stories high as it swooped an aerial course of arcs and figure-eights. "I weigh about 300 pounds and this thing was pulling me around with no problem," said Phillip Johnson. "You always feel the wind on your face so you know it can blow, but when you actually get that force to focus on your hands you get an appreciation for how concentrated it really is." Clemmons, seeing exactly that, was convinced she had identified the best type of kite for carrying heavy objects. The parafoils consistently kept their shape—and thus maintained their pull—regardless of the strength of the wind gusts. They were also easier to control than the deltas or the box kite, especially after the group had enough manpower guiding the line. The only question was whether they could control side-to-side swaying once a heavy object was attached.

Clemmons made a point of taking a long look at the soaring parafoil, then asked John and the others reel it back to earth—a considerable effort in its own right. For the first time, the laughter died down. Clemmons's theory no longer seemed trivial. The combination of strong wind, a parafoil that was difficult to control, and the prospect of trying to lift heavy objects meant there was a very realistic chance someone could be injured. At the same time, the TV cameras were now rolling and the journalists were ready to see whether Clemmons's theory literally carried any weight.

Sticking to her experiment agenda, Clemmons grabbed a ten-foot-long redwood beam she had found in Mara's backyard and coiled the nylon kite line around one end. She felt a lump in the back of her throat, not only because it was time for the first real test but because she was suddenly worried whether John and her friends could actually make the experiment happen without getting hurt. She felt overwhelmed, and noticed several of the men talking over her, shouting their ideas, ignoring what she had to say. The experiment hadn't even begun, she realized, and she could already feel it slipping from her control.

She assigned three people to take up positions on the left side of the park, and three others on the right. They were going to be the last defenses, either to protect straying pedestrians or grab any wayward kite lines that got away in the strong winds. People dickered over her instructions; some of them wanted to stay directly with the kites. Eventually she managed to get six people stationed at the edges, another at the far end of the field, and two standing on either side to control the beam during its ascent... if there was an ascent.

With the gusts increasing, Clemmons decided to hold off on the parafoils and start out with the delta kites, since that was what she had the most experience working with. She carried one of the deltas to a point several feet in front of the beam. Phillip Johnson had the other kite, and both were tied to the same end of the beam. Several people shouted orders, but Clemmons insisted on sticking with her initial plan: to simulate raising an obelisk from horizontal to an angle of forty degrees or more, using the beam in place of the obelisk. If that worked, she figured, they would proceed to phase two: lifting the log straight up.

All the voices quieted, or at least it seemed that way to Clemmons. She wasn't certain whether people were now worried, or just curious, or if she was so tense she blocked everything else out of her mind. All she knew was that suddenly all she could hear was her labored breathing and the furious wind gusts. She looked at Johnson, and they exchanged a silent acknowledgment that they were both ready. "Let it go," she told herself, but her fingers remained clamped around the kites, some small part of her still afraid of what might happen. Finally she took a deep breath, gave Johnson the word, and released the kites.

They shot up like rockets, pulling the line taut as they spun in mid-air, swooped down, and hit the ground. The beam hadn't moved, but then again there hadn't been a chance; the two kites never achieved a high enough angle to lift it. Clemmons thought she would just pick them up off the ground and try again, but the lines were tangled so badly it took more than ten minutes to get them straightened out. Everyone took their positions again, she gave Johnson the okay, and they released the deltas.

This time the deltas lifted skyward, and fast. The rope went taut and before Clemmons or Johnson had a chance to react the beam was angled up, four feet off the ground, pivoting like a pendulum gone wild. Clemmons let go of the kite line and jumped over the beam as it swung around, barely avoiding a slam in the ribs. The kite started dragging the beam downfield and went several yards before a bunch of the guys managed to catch up with it.

"Bring it down, bring it down!" she shouted to Johnson, as several other people ran to grab the line she had lost. The beam continued pivoting as the kites fluttered in different directions, and Clemmons could hear everyone shouting, struggling to pull them down. The whole thing only lasted about thirty seconds, but it seemed like forever. When the kites—and the beam—finally hit the ground, she yelled a victorious, "We lifted a redwood beam at an angle!"

It wasn't much of a victory, and she knew it. But it was precisely what she wanted to show her kids: the initial, tiny steps necessary when conducting a science experiment. And even though it was clear she needed more control, she now knew that a simple nylon kite could lift a redwood beam like it didn't weigh a thing.

She heaved a huge sigh of relief, grateful that no one got hurt. She decided never to attempt something like that again without control lines attached to the beam, to control side-to-side swaying. She looked over at the NBC crew, noticing they weren't exactly impressed, knowing that in their eyes she had seemingly added to the evidence that her theory was off the mark by showing how difficult it would be to control an airborne object. "It was pretty chaotic," David Bloom, the *Daily News* reporter, recalled later. "It was her sister, her husband, and an odd lot of kids, neighbors, cats and dogs that were out in some damn cold, blustery weather trying to figure out what they were doing. I think part of the problem was they really didn't know what they had, so when they found out they could lift something heavy they were like, 'oh my god, what do we do now that we've really got this thing in the air?' "

Nonetheless, from Clemmons's perspective the initial test was a success, albeit poorly and perhaps dangerously executed. She untwisted the kites and re-secured the line from the first delta around the end of the beam. Phillip

Johnson untangled the second kite's line and wrapped it around the opposite end of the beam. The concept for the second phase was simple, and visually appealing: to lift the beam straight up using the vertical pull from the kites attached to both ends. For the media, this was basically going to be the proof of Clemmons's pudding. If the beam went nowhere... so would the story.

Clemmons set everyone up just like before, only this time with two people holding each kite line instead of one. She looked at everyone's faces, knowing her months of research and investment money seemed to boil down to whether or not she could raise the redwood beam straight up, wishing the wind gusts weren't so violent. The she gave the signal to release the kites.

The beam rose off the ground, dipping up and down like a bucking bull, striking the ground as often as it launched into the air. Still, there was no denying the visual impact of seeing a heavy beam in mid-air, effortlessly hoisted by nothing more than a pair of four-foot-long, nylon kites. Clemmons let out a happy scream. The kites were lifting the beam so easily she and the others had to grab onto it to keep it from lifting too high off the ground. As she wrapped her hands around the beam she felt the pull of the wind, trying to carry her up. "I've finally met the Egyptians' invisible sky gods!" she joked.

Energized by her success, Clemmons was ready for a third experiment. This was the one she had been hoping for, the one where the obelisk came into play. Just getting it into the park was a challenge: it took four men to load the 400-lb. obelisk onto a furniture dolly and push it up the steep hill, prompting them to joke that it would have been easier to fly it to the top. Clemmons thought the joke was right on target; to her, the difficulty and her volunteers' reaction underscored her point that the Egyptians would not have undertaken such brutal work. Several members of the group, still huffing and puffing from moving the obelisk, readily agreed.

Unfortunately for Clemmons, that was the last time everyone was of one mind. Buoyed by their success at lifting the beam, the already opinionated group was now intent to direct the next experiment. Clemmons, determined to stick with the specific experiments and goals she outlined in advance, discovered that wasn't going to be an easy task given the group's sudden enthusiasm. She instructed the people hauling the obelisk to place it close to the bluff at the edge of the park, a technique that helped keep kite lines from tangling during her preliminary tests using the miniature obelisks. But this time she was out-shouted by several others who were convinced wheeling the obelisk to a down-wind position was a better option.

"There was a point that frustration set in, because the wind, more than the people, would be so uncooperative," Johnson said later. "You'd break three kite strings, the lines were twisting, and it was very difficult to communicate back and forth because you can't call to a person who's seventy yards away and have them hear you when the wind is so loud. The whole thing was very frustrating for Maureen, and for everybody. I think she had thought about everything in a broad sense, in terms of picking up the post and the obelisk and laying down the details of how to tie and control the kites, but she hadn't gone in any depth or detail about it. You'd come back in and she'd say we should have done this or that, slack off or tighten up, and people would say, 'we couldn't hear you so we didn't know.' There was a point where that became a real issue, and that led to a lot of ideas and recommendations."

In the end Clemmons conceded to the will of the group... but not happily. "It got to the point where all these men were running around barking orders at each other, each wanting to be the lead dog, but none of them had paid for any of the kites or spent any time on the research," John said. "Maureen was telling people she had done some earlier experiments with the kids, that she knew what she was doing, but they wouldn't listen. It seemed like there was this testosterone-driven mentality that she didn't know anything about manly stuff like ropes and how to lift big objects. I mean, here we were all out there because of Maureen, and they wouldn't listen to her because she was a woman. It was chaos."

John began barking Maureen's instructions, helping to restore order, and several members of the group finally stopped debating long enough to secure the main parafoil lines around the obelisk. Maureen, with some assistance, propped the obelisk at a forty-degree angle for the initial obelisk test. Her plan was to see whether the kites could lift the obelisk at all, and ideally if it could lift it up to a full ninety-degree standing position.

Securing the 400-lb. obelisk for an early field test.

Time and again, Clemmons gave directions but was either ignored or questioned every step of the way, and she was left bristling. She knew this was just backyard science, but she also wanted to handle things with specific procedures so she could track the kite angles, wind speeds and other pertinent information. That, she could tell, wasn't going to happen with the group at hand. She had lost control.

The experiment took forever, with dozens of re-starts as everyone shouted ideas and tried to cope with twisted lines, unpredictable winds and a dozen other setup complications. When everyone finally had a feel for the wind gusts and how to handle the parafoils, they reset the lines, got the kites into position downfield, and waited for a strong enough gust.

Clemmons felt the wind kick up against her cheeks. She raised her hand and shouted for the guys to release the parafoils. They shot skyward and her heart did too, because right before her eyes the nose of the 400-lb. obelisk—the same obelisk that was so heavy they could barely get it into the park—lifted right off the ground and onto its base, up to the full ninety degrees, in less than two seconds. A few seconds later the wind pulled the obelisk all the way over and started dragging it downfield. The experiment was a success: the obelisk's weight presented no obstacle whatsoever.

"We did it!" Clemmons screamed. "It worked! We did it!"

Better yet, they had done it for the news cameras. A group of amateurs had raised a 400-lb. obelisk fifty degrees in less than two seconds, using nothing but a kite and some nylon line. The implication seemed clear: wind power could indeed be used for engineering and construction. The size and weight of any given obelisk no longer mattered, because erecting a 200-ton obelisk would involve nothing more than taking what Clemmons had just learned—the importance of control, finding the right kite design, and identifying the right types of rope—and then mathematically extrapolating to a larger scale.

Kites lift the 400-lb obelisk in Wilbur-Tampa Park

That, she explained to her children in the aftermath, is science: failure, failure, failure, success… followed by many more failures and successes. She made certain the kids understood failure was part of the process, that you learn as much from the failures as from the successes.

The first of those subsequent failures came right away, when Clemmons and her group decided to jump ahead and lay the obelisk on the ground in hopes of raising it the full distance, from a supine position to a full vertical. This time, Clemmons hadn't done the math in advance; she didn't know what would happen. Sure enough, the parafoil lines snapped and the sails went flying down the field. One of them soared off and disappeared altogether. Clemmons had a back-up, but the subsequent attempt produced the same result. "Wow," John said. "I just watched several hundred dollars sail off into the distance."

Clemmons decided it was time to call it a day. She accomplished all but one goal and generated a wealth of information about handling kites attached to heavy objects. She now knew that 200-lb. test line was not strong enough to handle both the force of the wind and the weight of an obelisk. She also learned the knots that developed from strong wind twisting the lines were particularly damaging since the lines always snapped at the knotted points. And she had determined that the group's best work seemed to happen in a twenty-five mile-per-hour wind; anything more, and everything slowed down as lines twisted and the kite flailed. In terms of collecting data and demonstrating her concept, the day went almost exactly as she had hoped—an accomplishment the local media found admirable. "The most interesting part wasn't whether it had a thing to do with the pharaohs, it was how an idea could infect somebody with its power and compel them to get out of their relatively quiet, suburban life," said Bloom, the *Daily News* reporter. "Clemmons is a bright woman; she's got a degree in organization change, she was studying for her doctorate, she's got two kids, a loving husband, and worked as vice president of a large company... she had a pretty full life, with a lot going on, and yet this idea so overtook her brain that she made space for it and drove it. That field test was a wonderful illustration of the power of ideas."

Not everyone saw it that way. NBC's reporter told Clemmons the network would not air a story on the experiment unless she was able to lift the obelisk from a supine position. Perhaps the bigger problem, Clemmons later realized, was the fact the field test looked painfully amateur, which inadvertently undermined her accomplishments by making the success appear little more than random chance.

She drove to her office that afternoon and ordered two more parafoils and some 400-lb. nylon test line. The next morning, a reporter from the Fox television network's Los Angeles affiliate called to ask whether she could repeat the experiment for their cameras. As chance would have it, the parafoils and test line she'd just ordered arrived that afternoon—four days earlier than promised. Clemmons checked the windy weather forecast and saw another opportunity. No problem, she told the Fox reporter, and made plans to meet him in Wilbur-Tampa Park at 8 a.m.

She took to the phones that evening, calling all of her friends and family to ask for their help once again. She also made a point of having a long talk with the people who had caused the most trouble on Sunday—nothing nasty, but enough to make certain everyone would stick to carefully planned procedures rather than disputing instructions. She knew no one had meant anything personal when they bullied their opinions into the field test, they were just having a good time, asserting their ideas like anyone normally would with friends. But she also knew it had to stop if the project was to succeed.

Monday night was a repeat of Saturday night, a lot of sleepless hours followed by an early morning wake-up call. Maureen loaded up the Mitsubishi and drove to the park at 5:30 a.m. Only a couple of joggers were there, and with less than ten days until the winter solstice even the sun was taking its sweet time. She set up camp, unloading the three parafoils and a few of the basic materials, then waited. A wind check revealed a steady 25 mph breeze with gusts up to 30 mph—nothing close to the gusts of two days earlier. Since it was a weekday the kids would be in school and the crowd would be smaller. By 7:30 the sun was shining, eleven people had arrived, and the obelisk was already at the end of the park, near the bluff as she had intended on Sunday.

She attached the 400-lb. test line and ran it halfway down the park, a distance of about forty yards. This time she made a point of resting the nose of the obelisk on top of the overturned furniture dolly, to make sure the nose was level with the base. She also passed out walkie-talkies, for better communication, and fed the line attached to the obelisk through a hastily assembled pulley so the wind would lift the stone up without flipping it over.

Before the group attached the control lines to the kites, Clemmons gathered everyone together for an informal meeting. She reminded them that a news crew would be arriving and told them how unprofessional the scene they presented on Sunday had looked. She also asserted that since she was the source of the theory and the field tests, it was important that everyone take direction from her without objections, and without shifting any of the attention away from the goal of the tests. The only way results of her kite tests would make it beyond the grassy borders of Wilbur-Tampa Park, she explained, was to have the media get word to the public—something that was never going to happen unless everyone did things in an orderly fashion and acted like a team interested in science rather than just goofing around with kites in a park.

No one said anything—her words were so seeped in truth there was no need. Instead they just nodded and went to work. By the time the Fox crew showed up a half-hour later, the group had successfully conducted the experiment several times and knew the exact routine.

Five minutes after the cameras were set up, the group had the kites in the air and the obelisk lifted into an erect position, from zero to ninety degrees. The entire event looked as professional as a group of backyard scientists could make it. Best of all, Clemmons managed to demonstrate her point quickly, cleanly, and visually. The news crew was not only impressed, they found her work so captivating they chatted with Clemmons off-camera for an extended period of time, and asked to be kept apprised of any future field tests.

That night, she was so exhausted from the culmination of her months-long effort that she nearly fell asleep before Fox aired its segment, mid-way through the ten o'clock news. Once she watched, however, she was too excited to sleep. Maureen Johnson Clemmons, with no engineering degree, had managed to inject her innovative concept for pyramid construction into Los Angeles' popular thinking. Now it was just a matter of convincing the world of science to pick up the ball and run.

CHAPTER FOUR

The Evidence Mounts

P eople sometimes tell me I need to learn how to read the hieroglyphs, but most ancient Egyptians didn't know how to read. How do you communicate with people who can't read? Easy: hieroglyphs. Which tells you that unlocking their original meaning means ignoring modern convention and looking at things the way the ancient Egyptians would have seen them—as people who didn't know how to read. It's fun to think that the pharaohs adorned themselves with symbols for no other reason than the fact they were filthy rich and they could do it. It even kind of fits our modern, western view of the world. But it's a big mistake to assume everything they had was for show.

Field test results in hand, Clemmons sent news clips of her research efforts to several university Egyptologists, and even left phone messages for a few of them. While awaiting responses, she returned her thoughts to the ankh—the cross-like Egyptian hieroglyph repeatedly depicted in the claws of birds. Why, she wondered anew, wasn't the emblem on their wings, or in the sky, or anywhere else? Why always in the birds' claws? She reviewed what she knew from her research: the ankh was associated with "the breath of life." The symbol was also used to spell the ancient Egyptian word for "block of stone," and most of the ankh renderings in ancient Egyptian art featured something that looked like rope or twine around the crosspiece of the symbol. She thought back to the field tests, and how a 25 mph wind sent the kite line slicing right through her gloves, into her hands. Could the ankh be more than just a symbol?

She knew she needed a physical version of an ankh, one that would force her mind to stop thinking of it as a hieroglyph and look at it as an object instead. The search took several weeks—nature stores, garden shops, and museum art dealers had no idea where she could purchase one, and even the clerks at a head shop were in a haze over ankhs. Exasperated, Clemmons tried a New Age store. While scoffing at the crystals she did a double-take. There it was, the ankh she was looking for... sort of. The object in question was about the size of a small pipe wrench and fastened to a base, like a statue. Clemmons spent thirty-five dollars for the metallic statue, promptly unscrewed the ankh from the base, and held it up. It was perfect.

She took it home and looked at it from all angles, close up and at a distance. Nothing changed. The ankh was still basically a hand-held cross with a large, looping top. Then she felt it in her hand, closing her eyes, gauging the weight. She did everything she possibly could to stop thinking of the ankh as a symbol and try to open her mind to some other use. If it wasn't a symbol, how about... a tool?

She studied it some more. It certainly didn't resemble any tool she'd ever seen... except possibly a carabiner, the D-shaped, metallic hoop used to fasten a rock-climber's safety rope. Since Clemmons didn't know much about carabiners, she drove to a local sporting goods store, slapped the ankh on the counter, and—without saying what it was—asked a store clerk if he had ever seen anything like it. The guy picked it up, shrugged, and said, "Of course I've seen this before, it's some sort of rappelling tool." He took her over to a store display, grabbed a modern rappelling device, and held it up next to the ankh. The two instruments looked the same—a large loop with a hand-hold underneath.

Clemmons asked him to demonstrate how it worked without mentioning her version was an ankh. The clerk showed her how the device controls rope: you thread the rope through the head of the ankh, wrap it around the crosspiece, and then the rope cannot be pulled free regardless of how much force is applied. Flick the ankh the opposite direction, thus freeing the rope from the crosspiece, and suddenly the rope slides through the head freely.

Clemmons didn't believe him, so they tried an experiment right there in the store. The clerk grabbed some rope, and looped it through the ankh without wrapping it around the crosspiece. Then he gave her the other end of the rope. "Okay, pull it," he said. She did, and of course it slid through the looped head of the ankh right away. Then he put the rope through the ankh again, only this time he wrapped it around the crosspiece. She pulled: the rope didn't go anywhere. But as soon as he flicked his wrist, swiveling the ankh so that the crosspiece was directly in line with her hands, the rope loosened and pulled through the loop.

Clemmons, knowing she wasn't exactly Mrs. Olympia, figured she didn't have the strength to yank the rope through when he had the crosspiece angled the other direction. The clerk laughed when she said that and suggested they try again—only this time with more force. He snaked the rope through the head of the ankh, gave her the other end, and told her to run full-speed down the aisle, fast as she could. Clemmons glanced at the other people in the store, embarrassed, but took the rope and jogged down the aisle.

The rope pulled easily—then suddenly stopped, yanking her backwards from the force of the abrupt halt. She turned to see what had happened. The only thing the clerk had done was use his right hand to swivel the ankh, so the rope would catch around the crossbar. One simple twist had stopped the full force of her moving body. She grabbed the ankh and looked at it with newfound respect.

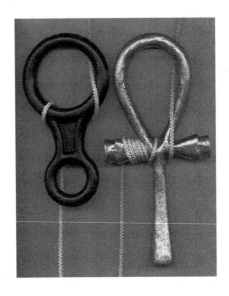

The ankh: symbol, or tool?

"Hieroglyphic symbol, my rear end!" she said. "This thing is a tool!"

Maybe, she realized, it was just what the store clerk suggested: the ancient equivalent of a contemporary rock-climber's safety carabiner. Or maybe... maybe it was the perfect tool to control a kite. Everyone knows the force of a strong wind at their backs, and the kind of tug a high wind can give you if you're hanging onto a kite line. Clemmons's own field test made it pretty obvious that control in high winds was a critical issue. With an ankh, the ancient Egyptians had the means for such control.

That weekend, Clemmons took her kids to the park and used the ankh to fly kites. It worked just as well, if not better, than any other line controller. When she drove home she could barely keep herself from bouncing up and down on the car seat. She spent the next several days looking at other common, ornamental items depicted in Egyptian art, wondering whether they too might be tools rather than symbols.

One possibility stood out: a javelin-style staff with a clawed top resembling the head of a pick-ax, known as the Scepter of Seth. When she showed a hand-held replica of the scepter to her office landlord—who just happened to hold a Ph.D. in engineering—he couldn't understand why the pharaohs were holding the device upside down. "It looks like a lever," he told Clemmons. "You wedge the rim of the claw-shaped part underneath something, then pull back on the handle. It'll lift the thing right up." Again Clemmons's mind raced. Could the so-called "scepters" have actually been levers, used to manipulate heavy stones?

Inspired, she took the replica scepter to Bob Jacobi, the owner of a building supply shop that specialized in brick and rock, who took one look and thought she was holding a crowbar. He led Clemmons outside to a pile of granite rocks, picked one that weighed about 500 pounds, then demonstrated how easy it was to torque the rock at a thirty-five-degree angle using a crowbar that matched the head of the scepter.

The critical element in calculating torque, Jacobi explained, was the length of the staff. He demonstrated how a hand-held device would not be efficient, but something "staff height" could be pulled from the shoulder rather than bending down and losing some of the pull. Clemmons, remembering her basic physics (torque is the product of force multiplied by length), agreed that it made sense. She returned to her museum replicas and noticed another scepter, known to Egyptologists as the B3 or SHM scepter. Jacobi, a mason, took one look at the scepter's shape and said, "It's a chisel." More specifically, the head of the scepter resembled a long-nosed chisel found on the shelves of most hardware stores. Clemmons checked the hieroglyphs and found images of both hand-held and staff-sized B3 scepters.

Of course, Clemmons knew that without some sort of corroboration from ancient Egyptian artifacts her ideas were nothing more than speculation—which is why her subsequent discovery seemed particularly relevant. After studying the head of a lotus scepter held in museum replicas of Hathor and Isis, Clemmons got the nagging feeling she had seen the same scepter before. It turned out she had: while reading through her pile of Egyptology books. She scanned the pages and found what she was looking for: an image of an ancient Egyptian mason's mallet in *Ancient Egyptian Construction & Architecture*, by Somers Clark and R. Engelbach. The mallet and the lotus scepter are virtually identical.

At that point, Clemmons felt as if she had turned a corner. While she knew Egyptologists and historians were good at their jobs, she also knew that they ultimately approached their studies from very similar, collective perspectives. If you ask Joe Homeowner what a hammer is for, he will tell you it's for pounding nails. Ask a building contractor, and suddenly it's a tool for pulling, knocking, and sometimes levering. Ask a writer, and it might very well be a paperweight. Everyone comes at things from their own perspectives, and few of us try to step outside of those perspectives. Clemmons was convinced there was a good chance Egyptologists were overlooking the possibility that ornamental items worn and carried by the gods in ancient Egyptian art could be reinterpreted as tools.

One morning she arrived at her office and found an email from a kite aficionado who had read about her research and wondered whether she knew that the Egyptians would have had to apply shellac to their linen kites in order to make them air-tight. Applying shellac to the linen would mitigate permeability, something Clemmons had not considered. Early biplane designers faced the same problem, since the biplanes were often made of linen and wood and designers thus had to apply doping agents to keep the linen airtight. That led to the question: would the ancient Egyptians have had access to some form of shellac or sealing dope?

Clemmons wasn't able to answer the kite aficionado's question because, like most of us, she had no idea where shellac comes from. A little Internet research turned up an answer: shellac is made from the exudate of scale insects such as the lac beetle. That flagged Clemmons's attention right away, because while she didn't know anything about lac beetles she did know that scarab beetles are featured very prominently in ancient Egyptian art.

She contacted Michael Klein, an entomologist at the US Department of Agriculture, who confirmed lac beetles do in fact produce exudate and invited her to be a guest speaker at a convention of scarab beetle entomologists. She told him flat out: she didn't know a thing about beetles. Klein laughed and said he just wanted her to present the wind engineering theory, mentioning the possible role of the beetles.

She did, and the entomologists went wild with excitement, barraging her with questions. Conference organizers had trouble getting the researchers to sit down—they were too busy scrutinizing the hieroglyphs and talking. Maybe, everyone agreed, the beetles weren't depicted in Egyptian artwork for their ornamental appearance but because the Egyptians used them to manufacture a substance similar to shellac—an intriguing possibility since many of the beetle depictions suggest dark brown effluent emanating from the hind-end of the beetle into a vessel or bowl.

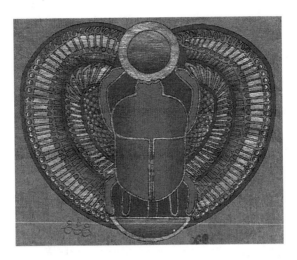

*Beetles in ancient Egyptian art: commonplace,
ornamental... and useful?*

Organizers started flicking the conference lights on and off, but the entomologists still wouldn't sit down. Clemmons, baffled, said, "You people are the premier scarab entomologists in North America—hasn't any Egyptologist ever asked you what the scarab beetles in the hieroglyphs meant?" They all shook their heads and said, "Nope." Stunned, she asked, "Why hasn't an Egyptologist ever asked an entomologist what this means?" No one had an answer.

A few weeks later, with some guidance from the entomologists, Clemmons had her children working with Los Angeles' green peach beetles, using paintbrushes to tease the insects' hind ends, triggering the gooey excretions that the insects use as a defense mechanism. It was, hands down, an incredibly gross backyard science project... so of course, the kids loved it. Clemmons had them paint the beetle exudates across linen mounted on an embroidery hoop, then tested the results using blow dryers. Sure enough, uncoated linen let the wind blow right through; the exudates-coated linen blocked the breeze.

She later conveyed those findings, and the others, in a research paper she presented at a meeting of the International Society of Educators and Scholars (ISES), an organization of college and university instructors. Feature articles about her efforts appeared in *The Los Angeles Times Magazine* and on the ABC News website. The Discovery Channel phoned, asking to film her next field test. A Michigan retiree with a degree in ion physics called to offer his assistance. Closer to home, a mother of four children called because her ten-year-old daughter wanted to participate in the field tests as part of a school science project. During a business meeting at MGM, one of the studio's managers perked up and asked Clemmons if she was "the wind lady."

The only contingent with zero interest, it seemed, was Egyptologists. Despite emailing, phoning and faxing the Egyptology and archaeology departments at several universities, she failed to attract a single returned message. David Bloom, the Los Angeles *Daily News* writer who attended the field tests, ran into the same problem when he tried contacting Egyptologists for some informed opinions. "I went through this lengthy process of calling most of the Egyptology places that matter—the museums in New York, the Smithsonian, the Fields, several archeology departments at major universities—trying to figure out whether what Clemmons was saying made sense scientifically and was historically accurate," Bloom said. "But I never really got anyone to comment. Getting an Egyptologist turned out to be a major pain in the ass."

For the first time since Clemmons started her project, she wasn't sure what to do. Assembling another round of field tests on her own, using larger kites and heavier obelisks, wasn't an option. She didn't have the money or the location, and she wasn't about to have someone risk their life trying to lift a massive rock in a park. She knew that somehow, some way, she needed to find professionals to oversee the project, so she applied for research grants from various private and public research sponsors, including the J. Paul Getty Trust and the National Science Foundation. Snare some research money, she figured, and even stubborn scientists will notice what you are doing. Again, she hit a wall: representatives for the NSF and others told her very succinctly that non-PhD, unpublished researchers rarely receive grants.

Even as her efforts failed, other battlefronts formed around her. She was studying for comprehensive EdD exams at Pepperdine University, writing her dissertation, working as full-time business consultant for three large companies... and raising two children. In the midst of it all, her mother suffered a seizure and was rushed to the hospital. Her father-in-law, Jack Clemmons, suffered a ruptured aorta and passed away three weeks later—a particularly tough blow since Maureen and Jack were extremely close. Exhausted, Clemmons started to second-guess herself, wondering whether the kite project was too much of a challenge, sapping time and energy she could otherwise spend with her family.

Just as she was feeling it might be time to lay the wind engineering theory to rest, a new message arrived in her email box. Her eyes widened as she saw it was from Hans Hornung, director of the California Institute of Technology's aeronautical laboratory, and they widened even further when she saw that the subject line read "Kite Theory."

Clemmons had sent Hornung several email messages telling him about her theory. She had also sent him "snail mail" copies of her ISES paper, and spoken with his receptionist on several occasions. To that point, there had never been any real response—only a couple of polite brush-offs from his secretary. Now, Dr. Hornung had taken the time to write a message. Clemmons already knew from months of cold-calling that most researchers never bothered to return messages... why would they, unless...

She opened the message and grinned as she read, "Your project sounds quite interesting. I have forwarded your message to (emeritus) Professor Anatol Roshko, who is undoubtedly the most expert person for this particular sort of fluid mechanics." Clemmons, wearing a big smile, had to resist the urge to throw the computer mouse into the air and scream in triumph. She messaged Roshko, who asked whether she was interested in coming to campus to discuss her ideas in detail. They agreed on a date and time, and as Clemmons shut down her computer that evening she let out the yell that had been begging to escape. After a two-year struggle, she had finally landed a meeting with a scientist from one of the top engineering universities in the world—a scientist whose opinion would make or break the kite theory once and for all.

CHAPTER FIVE

The Meeting

I've given a lot of presentations before, but this one was different. I took a deep breath, and after that I don't remember breathing for twenty minutes. I just slowly outlined everything: the kites, the field tests, even the history and climate of Egypt. I had one of the engineers stand up and try out the ankh, so they could experience its usefulness as a tool for restraint and control of heavy lines and weights. I really put my heart and soul into that presentation.

Finally I paused, and that's when I got nervous. It hit me in the gut right then: these guys were going to start asking questions, and I was going to have to defend myself against five of Caltech's top engineers. That was the moment when the fear finally set in. It was all going to come down to whether or not I *could survive a question-and-answer session with these great thinkers.*

Truth be told, Clemmons felt intimidated from the moment she set foot on the California Institute of Technology campus, which lacks the stately architecture of an Ivy League institution but conveys academic intimidation through building placards, art, and other subtle reminders of its twenty-eight Nobel Prize winners. The fact Linus Pauling and Richard Feynman once wandered the tree-lined quads made Clemmons feel like a rookie outfielder assigned to patrol Babe Ruth's old spot in Yankee Stadium.

She met Roshko, a slender, clean shaven man with light hair, and he quickly informed her that "the others" were waiting in a nearby room. Clemmons hesitated, thinking, "Others?" She followed him into a conference room that looked like something beige exploded. The walls were beige, the floor was beige, even the conference table was beige. The only things that weren't beige were the four people sitting at the table. Roshko introduced her to Hans Hornung, the man who had initially replied to her email, and three other department engineers.

At first Clemmons didn't know what to say. She looked at the group of engineers sitting in front of her, not spread around the table but five in a row, and couldn't help thinking the scene looked like a military tribunal. As Roshko explained the basic concept of the wind engineering theory to the others, Clemmons wheeled her portable luggage trolley to the table and started unpacking the miniature obelisk, the ankh, samples of the kites she'd used for the field tests, photos of the hieroglyphs, and every scrap of research she had put together.

There was an awkward silence when Roshko finished talking; Clemmons wasn't certain how to begin. Roshko made it easy: he simply told her to go ahead. "She clearly wasn't a professional in the field," says Roshko, "but I had seen the same Nova program about the failed attempt to raise an obelisk, and the idea of using a kite to do the job seemed interesting." Hornung was thinking much the same thing. "I didn't look through everything she sent to me, but I had read her basic idea when she first sent it, and there was enough to it that I wanted to hear more," he says. "We were interested to see if we could help her check this out."

Clemmons outlined everything. Finally she stopped, stared at the five faces and, not really knowing what else to say, asked the inevitable question. "So... what do you think?" The dreaded moment had arrived. She now needed to defend her wind engineering concept against five Caltech engineers.

Then something remarkable happened. There was no barrage of questions. No dead silence. No 'thank-you-very-much-we'll-be-in-touch.' Instead the five engineers ignored her and began talking amongst themselves, sounding excited. They doodled some math on their scratch pads. They laughed, shrugged, and nodded in affirmation. For three or four minutes, Clemmons didn't even exist. Then one of the engineers turned to her and said, "You know, this idea works."

They started talking again. "All you need to upright a thousand-ton obelisk," Roshko told them while running through some quick calculations, "is a twenty-five mile per hour wind." Clemmons looked at him and said, "Don't you want to start with a two-ton stone first—the size the Nova team used?" Roshko shook his head. "That's too easy," he said. "I already know we can do that."

Clemmons let out a celebratory whoop. Startled, and concerned that their comments had been misconstrued as an endorsement, the engineers quickly established that they were only interested in wind engineering—not pyramid construction. "I was intrigued, but it's a long way between possibility and proof," Roshko says. "Although there's nothing in the aerodynamics of wind engineering that would make it impossible, there are other things that make me skeptical. With all we know about ancient Egypt, all the records and the pictures, there's no clue that kites were ever used. I thought that was hard to get by. But from an engineering standpoint, what she was suggesting didn't seem to be an impossible idea, and we were impressed that she had already gone out with a small obelisk and a kite and demonstrated it on that small scale."

Most important, he and his colleagues liked the mathematics behind her idea. "We didn't actually go very deeply into the mechanics at that point, we just estimated some numbers and agreed that it could work," Hornung says. "We could tell that the forces you could exert with a kite would be enough to raise an obelisk. It was just a question of, could we control things well."

He and Roshko agreed that the matter was worth investigating. "Whether the Egyptians actually did it or not... who knows?" Roshko says. "The question at the time was, is there anything that would make what Clemmons was suggesting impossible on a bigger scale? I guess I basically told her what she wanted to hear: that it wasn't impossible, and it was worth looking into."

But while everyone thought the concept merited further study, no one felt motivated to champion the cause in an effort to secure research funds. The sobering fact, they told Clemmons, is that it costs thousands of dollars just to produce a mathematical model of a project. For a report and an actual field test, the costs would climb even higher. The precise estimates, they said, couldn't be worked up until someone determined the exact course of study necessary—important evaluative steps which also cost money. Clemmons shrugged it off and told them she would find financial sponsors, figuring that at some point it would be up to her to raise research money whether Caltech signed on or not.

Several days later Roshko called to let her know he and Hornung had discussed the project and felt that Morteza Gharib, one of the engineers at the lunch and a specialist in vortex dynamics, had the academic credentials best suited for the project. "This idea is in a subsonic, high Reynolds number flow field, and Mory Gharib is our local expert in this area," Hornung said. Clemmons wasn't thrilled with the plan; she had discussed the project at length with Roshko and enjoyed working with him. She also couldn't help but wonder whether Roshko was trying to dump the project on another colleague.

Then she met with Gharib and understood why Hornung and Roshko felt he was the best researcher for the job. Not only was Gharib accustomed to applying his background in fluid dynamics to real-world applications such as heart valves and naval vessels, his quiet nature and subdued, level-headed approach seemed an appropriate contrast to Clemmons's outgoing, gung-ho personality. Best of all, he had a genuine curiosity about her concept of using kites for heavy lifting. "I have an interest in technologies that ancient engineers may have used—not mechanical technologies but fluid-mechanical, like wings or vertical windmills," Gharib says. "Maureen's idea was interesting because it was quite out of range, and what attracted me was not whether the Egyptians did it or not, it was more the engineering challenge." True to form, Clemmons could barely contain her excitement during the meeting and made a point of bringing a camera so she could pose for photos with Gharib and the others while on campus.

Gharib, though skeptical about Clemmons's Egyptology "evidence," felt the idea of ancient civilizations using wind was not necessarily out of the question. "Engines do not lift planes, it's the air flow, so with the right wind speed and the right area, you can lift just about anything," Gharib says. "That's why I felt that if her idea worked it would happen through vortex flow—the flow separation behind a kite that can create a huge force."

He also knew that the concept required more than just kites and a determined group of people. The kite system needed a control method—something Clemmons wasn't surprised to hear since she had discovered that firsthand while trying to manipulate airborne objects during her field tests. "I also did not agree that you could use straightforward, standard kites like Maureen had used in the experiments she had done," Gharib says. "You need to have a large surface area to lift something heavy, and to structurally support a large surface area can be difficult, even with technology today. I don't think the Egyptians could have structurally built a kite that big. That meant there had to the right mix of efficient vortex flow and a system for control."

But Gharib, already swamped with his regular projects, also knew that without any research funds he couldn't assign the initial task—assembling mathematical models to explain the concept—to his graduate assistants. That basically left Gharib with one option: find a student willing to adopt it as a summer research project. In early 1999—five months after the first meeting at Caltech—Gharib called Clemmons with the good news that Emilio Graff, an undergraduate sophomore studying aeronautics, would compile the mathematical models while attending Caltech's Summer Undergraduate Research Fellowship (SURF) program.

The results were ready in October. Gharib hinted to Clemmons that he and Graff had come up with a "surprise" solution to the issue of how to control the kites and invited Clemmons to watch Graff present his SURF report to faculty advisors. When she arrived, she found the presentation site was another of the school's bland, beige rooms, only this time the desks and tables had been arranged in a horseshoe fashion, with an overhead projector in the center. By the time Graff began his presentation nearly forty people were packed into the room, many of them standing along the side walls or tucked into the corners. Several had nothing to do with the SURF program; sheer curiosity had drawn them to hear Graff's results.

In his report, Graff used mathematics and aerodynamic principles to outline two possible methods for erecting an obelisk using a kite: either with the kite tied directly to the obelisk, or tied to the obelisk in companion with an additional means of control. For both methods, he used specifications from eleven large obelisks to formulate generalized data for a large obelisk's center of mass and its rotational inertia as it swivels around its bottom edges. For the kites, he estimated aerodynamic force using a coefficient of lift and drag, the cross-section of the kite's surface area, and the density and velocity of air, factoring in the tension and mass of the kite string.

As it turned out, Graff's math demonstrated exactly what Clemmons had noticed during her field tests: the higher the angle of the kite, the less force is needed to lift an obelisk from a horizontal position. Graff also discovered that when the kite is flying at a non-vertical angle, the force requirement drops steadily as the obelisk is lifted further away from a horizontal position. "That means that if the force is constant, the obelisk will accelerate as it is lifted," Graff told the assembled crowd. "It poses a big problem: how do you stop an accelerating obelisk that weighs up to 500 tons?"

The closer a kite flew to ninety degrees, on the other hand, the closer the force requirement remains to the initial value throughout the raising—meaning an obelisk's acceleration is minimized. Since no kite can fly at ninety degrees—that would mean the kite was producing zero drag—Graff suggested the best method for raising a heavy obelisk using kites would be to erect a wood-beamed support tower over the nose of the obelisk, then channel the kite lines down to the obelisk through the center of the tower. The tower—a scaffold similar to an oil-drilling rig—would keep the lower portion of the kite lines at a ninety-degree angle, maintaining a vertical pulling force, while the kites could fly at angles, in shifting winds, without dragging the obelisk. The base of the obelisk, meanwhile, would be situated atop a small sled that would slide towards the center of the tower as the kite pivoted the nose of the obelisk upwards. "The Egyptians used sleds to transport the obelisks," Graff said, "so this is not as farfetched as it seems."

Graff's tower concept had a historical precedent: Italian architect Domenico Fontana utilized a 92-foot-tall wooden tower in concert with nine hundred men and seventy-five horses to raise the 200-ton Vatican Obelisk in 1586. While making calculations, however, Graff discovered a large problem: lifting the Vatican Obelisk using such a system would require 151 five-by-ten foot kites, which defies common sense. Even if the kites were each a much larger 10 X 20, the process would still require thirty-eight kites. Clemmons shifted uncomfortably in her seat as she listened to Graff say, "Clearly this suggests this is not a practical way to do it at all."

But Graff wasn't finished—and neither was Clemmons's theory. He pointed out that the way to overcome using a large number of kites was to use wind power more efficiently, then revealed the surprise that Gharib had hinted. "Pulleys are the answer," Graff said. "They provide a mechanical advantage, so we can reduce the amount of force we have to put into the system." Under Graff's plan, the scaffold tower would feature a set of pulleys on a fixed frame above the top pivot, near the tip of the obelisk. The result would be a simple block-and-tackle device that used kites to supply energy rather than using them to generate force. Such a design, Graff estimated, meant four five-by-ten kites flying three-quarters of a mile high in a 25 mph wind could lift the Vatican Obelisk in just a few minutes. In addition, the weight of the obelisk would be divided among the kites and the pulleys, and because there were only four kites and better controls the process would not require a large number of people to accomplish. The system even improved performance in conditions with changing wind speed, since any drop in kite power would be divided by the mechanics of the pulley system.

During his research, Graff had attempted to document the results of using such a system, going to the extent of constructing a seven-foot-tall scaffold tower near an undergraduate dorm with the intent of using it to raise Clemmons's 400-lb. obelisk. Campus pranksters had other ideas; Graff awoke one morning to news that the tower had been toppled and destroyed. Since there was no time to build another before his results were due, Graff recommended in his report that any further phase of research should begin with construction of another scaffold with a system of moveable pulleys that could first be used to lift Clemmons's obelisk before advancing to even heavier structures. "Although the idea of erecting obelisks with kites seems farfetched," Graff said, "the use of a system that provides a mechanical advantage yields not only positive but astounding results. From what I have found, it is clear that using kites with the pulley method is not only possible, but promising. And if it seems dubious that the Egyptians ever had kites, then who is to say they did not just put their boats on rollers and pull the obelisks up with those?"

Clemmons met with Graff and Gharib after the presentation and thanked them for their work, but didn't tell them she was riddled with mixed emotions. On the one hand she enjoyed hearing her concept validated, even if only on a very preliminary level. But hearing that they would need to use pulleys and a sled wasn't so exciting. Her concept had always been kites and stones, and even though she knew she needed a control system her gut feeling was that the ancient Egyptians would keep things as simple as possible, because of limitations in technology and the fact so few of the people could read. In that sense, she figured, Graff's idea was fine—pulleys are not a complicated form of machinery, and the Egyptians obviously understood basic engineering and math concepts. Still, she found herself unable to let go of the more simplistic kites and stones concept.

Eventually she reassured herself that Graff wasn't saying the Egyptians didn't raise stones by flying kites, just that they would have planned it out well in advance. Checking her research, she also learned that evidence of ancient Egyptian pulleys was discovered in the 1930s: a mushroom-shaped stone featuring three parallel grooves. At the time, archeologist Selim Hassan suggested the ancient Egyptians ran ropes through the notches while the stone was anchored within a scaffold or some other structure.

From Gharib's point of view, it didn't matter whether the ancient Egyptians used pulleys or not. "I have no intention to prove whether the Egyptians used this method," he said. "My intentions are just to use all means to see if this can be done from an engineering point of view. Whether they did it or not, that's a different story." Gharib told Clemmons he would proceed with the tower and the experiments as soon as they secured funding to do so. What he didn't tell her was how his opinion of her had begun to change. She wasn't an engineer, and Gharib knew it, but he couldn't help but think she also wasn't the novelty that he and his peers had considered her when they first met. "One thing that's very peculiar about her is that when you tell her something in conversation she always sends an email a couple of hours later that shows she obviously grasped the conversation and then went out and checked into it for herself," Gharib says. "She'll find a picture or a drawing in a book and say, 'Is this what you mean, does this support your idea?' She gives you what we call a feedback ratio of more than one. I wish some of my graduate students were like her, because you give her an idea and before you know it she comes back with many more ideas."

Clemmons was thrilled that Gharib was focused on the engineering rather than the ancient Egyptians. Bottom line, he had endorsed the physics behind her idea, and put a tentative stamp of approval on the concept of using kites to hoist massive objects. If the kites needed a companion system of pulleys to help do the job, then so be it—she could always demonstrate her fundamental kites-and-stones concept in the future.

In the meantime, she had managed to take her idea from her backyard to the point where Caltech aeronautics engineers agreed that the mathematical model was feasible. Now they needed to construct the new system and use it to lift a massive obelisk.

Which meant Clemmons still had a big problem: she needed to help Gharib find funding.

CHAPTER SIX

An Egyptologist Weighs In

I *can't be the first person to think of using the wind for lift. I just can't. I mean, sure, it's nice to think you're some kind of amazing pioneer, but history always proves you wrong. There are too many smart people out there.*

If that's true, it means someone else has tried something similar to what I'm doing. Maybe their work had nothing to do with the Egyptians, but there had to be someone who realized wind was an amazing tool for hoisting heavy objects. Even as I researched my way through book after book, turning up nothing, I just knew I couldn't be alone in this. I just knew there had to be someone else out there with a similar idea.

Imagine my surprise when I found out that someone was one of the greatest innovators of all time.

As Clemmons searched for investors, she also continued studying the lift potential of kites and discovered she had a historical ally: Alexander Graham Bell.

Bell, best known for inventing the telephone, was equally occupied by hopes of pioneering the first airplane. In the late 1890s, Bell hypothesized that a strong kite with large dimensions would have enough lift capability to carry a man and an engine across the sky. With that in mind, he spent the better part of ten years testing the lift capabilities of unique kite designs ranging from circular to polygonal to triangular. Bell soon became history's quintessential backyard scientist, working with his wife, Mabel, and as many volunteers as he could get to help him test kites near his home on Cape Breton Island, Nova Scotia. When the wind calmed, the group did what any home-based science team would do: they improvised, using a galloping horse to lift the kites instead.

Eventually Bell settled upon a honeycomb design with a series of tetrahedral cells, which seamstresses covered in thousands of yards worth of colorful silk. In 1905, Bell successfully used a 1,300-cell kite dubbed *Frost King* to lift 227 pounds of weight into the air—sixty-two pounds of rope, a rope ladder, and a 165-lb. man clinging to the ladder.

Two years later Bell built the *Cygnet,* a 40-foot-wide, 208-lb. kite that was so large it had to be loaded onto a barge and launched using a steam ship to tug the kite at high speed. Bell wanted to give the *Cygnet* a trial run prior to installing the engine, so on December 6, 1907, US Army Lieutenant Thomas E. Selfridge volunteered to crawl into the center of the kite and lay on his stomach as the accompanying steamer chugged across Cape Breton's Baddeck Bay. According to accounts of the experiment in National Geographic, the *Cygnet* rose off the barge and quickly soared to a height of 168 feet as Selfridge, who had no means of flight control, held on. Selfridge ended up flying for seven minutes—a feat unparalleled at the time.

Bell had erased any lingering doubts over whether a kite had the ability to haul heavy weight. His next planned step—attaching an engine to the kite—might well have placed Bell into the history books again except for one glitch: crewmen on the steam ship, their mouths agape at the sight of a man flying, forgot to sever the *Cygnet's* towrope as the kite settled on the water. As a result the *Cygnet* was dragged and destroyed, effectively concluding Bell's work with kites. [Selfridge survived, but ironically became powered flight's first fatality a few years later, when he was killed during an Army test of a Wright brothers-style aircraft.]

For Clemmons, Bell's work was further indication that her idea was feasible. Kites clearly had the ability to lift large amounts of weight, and no one questioned Bell's reputation as a scientist. Clemmons hoped that an expert in ancient Egyptian culture, presented with a neat trifecta of the physics, the math, and Bell's research, might be willing to take up the investigation. But Egyptologists remained as elusive as the buried artifacts they seek.

The field's history offers some explanation. Legends about the pyramids blossomed in the fifth century AD, after the last people capable of reading hieroglyphic script perished. By the time the Arabs conquered Egypt in 642 AD, the pyramids were no longer perceived as merely the tombs of kings but the locations of hidden, magical treasures. When French scholars discovered the Rosetta stone, they inadvertently fueled mysticism driven by myths reincarnated in hieroglyphs. The Great Pyramid, in particular, has allegedly served as a gigantic sundial, a landing reference for alien spaceships, and a marker for the intersection of the thirtieth parallel with the thirteenth meridian (an arbitrary system of measurement created long after the pyramids themselves). The purported methods for constructing the pyramid are equally, well... creative.

In essence, Egyptologists have been driven to cover by centuries of dubious, fanatical pyramid construction ideas. Granting even one amateur theory their attention, they feel, merely encourages others. Clemmons's letters and phone calls to Egyptologists would go unanswered and reporters' inquiries would be cast aside, not necessarily because of the theory itself but because that had become standard operating procedure.

Nothing changed until December, 1999, when *Time* published "How Do You Build a Pyramid? Go Fly a Kite." The story gave an overview of Clemmons and her theory, noting the usual reticence from Egyptologists. Mark Lehner, the renowned archaeologist whose work inspired Clemmons, declined comment—and he wasn't alone. But for the first time, a leading Egyptologist offered the scientific ammunition to balance Clemmons's theory with known facts.

Zahi Hawass, who at the time was under secretary of state for Egypt's Giza Plateau and director of the pyramids, disagreed with Clemmons' theory... but he listened to the details before pronouncing judgment.

"People have all kinds of ideas, and many of them are very entertaining, like this one," Hawass said. "But in science you have to go by the evidence. There is no evidence of kites at the pyramids. What we do have is the actual archeological remains of levers, ramps and rollers." Even if the kite remains had disintegrated over time, Hawass suggested, there would be another indication of their presence—artwork, mathematical schematics, etc. Hawass did not feel Clemmons's interpretations of the ankh, the wings atop the Egyptian monuments, the images of scarab beetles, or the mallet/scepter of Seth similarities held merit. "People see what they want to see," he said. "It's fantasy, or maybe science fiction. Every month someone comes to my office with a 'new way' of viewing the hieroglyphs. There's something about ancient Egypt that makes people think crazy things, but that's not what we [Egyptologists] are here to do. We're here for science, which means we take evidence and make conclusions based on that evidence. We don't sit back and imagine things."

Asked why Egyptologists seemed reluctant to talk, Hawass introduced the term "pyramidiots"—the profession's pet name for amateur Egyptologists. "You won't find many Egyptologists who will discuss something like [Clemmons's theory]," he said. "It's entertaining to think there's a conspiracy of some kind, and the pyramidiots all love to think that's what's happening. But we just don't have the patience for it anymore. It's tiring to have to take time out from your work to talk about crazy ideas when there is no mystery to how the pyramids were built. We have all the evidence right here, at the pyramids."

Hawass was right—Clemmons had no firm archaeological evidence, only theories and her own customized interpretations of hieroglyphs and friezes. While she had certainly opened up an interesting field of aeronautical research, the Egyptology side of her research was entirely debatable. The science of archaeology is indeed based upon evidence, and while Clemmons's interpretations were compelling they would never sway professionals.

But his comments also raised a question: did anyone really have any conclusions, other than the fact that Egyptologists and Clemmons disagreed with one another? Sure, there was plenty of evidence of levers, ramps and rollers... but Clemmons had said that from day one, and she never disputed that the ramps and rollers were part of the process. All she had suggested was they didn't comprise the *entire* process. As Hawass and others said, there was no direct evidence of kites in ancient Egypt... but common sense tells you that if a culture knows how to use linen sails to propel its boats, they certainly understand how wind works—and they understand that smaller versions of their sails could be fashioned and controlled from land.

Hawass had said it himself: "People see what they want to see." Clemmons wondered: couldn't that be applied to his Egyptology colleagues as well? It was one thing to go by hard evidence of ramps and rollers, but to rely solely on that evidence without looking at the whole picture seemed the equivalent of questioning whether a falling tree makes noise when no one is around. Technically it can't be proven... but apply some common sense and the answer is clear.

Frustrated, Clemmons took stock of the situation, suddenly aware that short of someone yanking a kite from underneath a pyramid she had no chance of getting an Egyptologist to take her concept seriously. The question, in her mind, was whether it mattered. Did she really need an Egyptologist's endorsement? Maybe not, since Caltech had already verified, at least on paper, that kites have tremendous lift capabilities. She also knew, on a gut level, that an ancient culture routinely sailing boats would almost certainly consider such an obvious natural resource for hoisting large objects. And she knew that even today, modern researchers have only managed to build tiny renditions of the pyramids. That suggested a missing element—some ingredient to the construction process that the researchers hadn't found. If she could get Caltech the funding to demonstrate the engineering side, the Egyptologists could remain as hard-nosed as they wanted and it wouldn't really matter. The engineering and construction communities, not to mention the public, would judge for themselves.

Did the Egyptians use kites to help build the pyramids? No one knows... including Egyptologists, whether they want to admit it or not. Which meant, Clemmons figured, the only way to get them to take a closer look was to team up with Caltech's engineers and show the Egyptologists how it was done.

CHAPTER SEVEN

Buddy, Can You Spare A Few Hundred Grand?

H ave you ever had one of those moments where someone told you something stunning, but you had to pre-
tend it was of no significance? I can top it.

I was at another meeting at Caltech, only this time the topic wasn't the legitimacy of my theory, it was how to actually prove it. Doing so required a full-scale demonstration using a scaffold and a really large obelisk—that much I already knew. I also knew it wouldn't come cheap. Still, I somehow never grasped just how not-cheap it was going to be. So I held my *breath and smiled as Mory calmly said, "We think we can do the whole thing for about $342,000."*

I'm a businesswoman, and I do okay for myself and my family – that's the reason I've been able to advance this theory even though there were times during this long process that I wondered how we were going to make ends meet. But $342,000? That was way above my budget. Heck, that was astronomically above my budget. Still, I just smiled and nodded. I'd come this far. There had to be a way.

Cutting corners wasn't much of an option. In Caltech's initial cost estimate, the materials alone amounted to nearly $28,000, and that was merely for computer services, data acquisition, equipment rentals, miscellaneous supplies, and graphic arts services. In addition, Gharib and his colleagues estimated that renting time in the school's wind tunnel—a process required to validate the aerodynamics of the kites in conjunction with the pulleys prior to constructing the scaffold—would require more than 470 hours and a grand total of at least $7,000, plus another $4,500 for the electricity to power the tunnel.

Labor costs consumed much of the remainder of the estimate. Caltech broke the project into three phases: the pre-test phase, which amounted to plan development, research relating to ancient technologies, and development of scale models and their accompanying balance systems. That, and preparing the related documentation, would be followed by a second phase which involved field and wind tunnel tests of the models to collect force and moment data and fine-tune methods for optimizing air flow over the surface of the kites. The third phase, dubbed a "post-test" phase, involved construction of full-scale models of the obelisk, tower, and kites, then field testing and documenting the system.

Clemmons read the estimate and felt as if she had just taken a belt to the gut. Her exasperation deepened when she noticed the estimate included a note warning of a five percent increase in labor costs the following fiscal year. As if that wasn't bad enough, Gharib sent her an update two weeks later in which he added an additional $50,000 to the estimate—the cost of consulting additional faculty members beyond the scope of the initial design, analysis, and field testing costs included in the earlier estimate.

Her first thought: find a corporate sponsor. A few years earlier, while working as senior buyer for a division of the 7-Eleven convenience store chain, she helped negotiate sponsorships and joint partnerships with the likes of Anheuser-Busch, Philip Morris, and Coca Cola. But funding a science experiment proved a tougher sell. Airborne Express and the Xerox Corp. considered Clemmons's proposal at length, but ultimately declined. Over the course of a year, Clemmons sent funding proposals to more than thirty of the country's largest corporations, as well as dozens of smaller companies and a handful of private investors, all to no avail. The names on what she called "TBNT" letters—"thanks, but no thanks"—read like a who's who of business: Microsoft, Boeing, Northwest Airlines, Philips Petroleum, The Coca Cola Company, Miller Brewing Company, Anheuser-Busch, Goodyear Rubber & Tire Co., Oracle, Dow Chemicals, Mitsubishi… the letters kept coming and coming. Even organizations with loose marketing ties to ancient Egypt, such as the Luxor Hotel in Las Vegas, turned her down, as did the Drachen Foundation—a non-profit organization that funds historical and cultural research involving kites.

Caltech's Gharib encountered the same fundraising difficulties. "Nobody wanted to be the first to invest," he says. "They always wanted someone else to do it first; after that, they said, they'd come in with their millions. But that didn't get us going."

Frustrated, Clemmons returned to her grassroots efforts, speaking at chamber of commerce meetings, Masonic lodges, or wherever she could drum up support. But by that time the kite-obelisk project wasn't her only worry—in fact, it wasn't even her primary worry. Six months before raising funds for the project became an issue, Clemmons left her job to launch her own hair care products company, meaning the business needed a healthy dose of startup capital. Eventually her desperation to fund the kite-obelisk project dovetailed with her desperation to fund the business. The result: continuous financial pressure, so much that she reached a point where she didn't know how she could possibly scrape by. For nearly two years her daily routine was a high-pressure formula: workdays at her company, a few hours being Mom, more work after the kids went to bed, a few hours of sleep, more work before the kids woke up in the morning, then back to the company again.

She developed red stress spots on her back, legs and face; she paced around her home at two in the morning, overwhelmed by her financial hurdles. John suggested it might be time for her to back away from the wind project, which would at least free up a few hours, but she refused.

With the pressure snowballing, Clemmons decided it was time to stop hunting for sponsors and take matters into her own hands. Turning to her beauty industry contacts and a couple of former college classmates, she swung a deal to manufacture a custom cologne packaged in pyramid-shaped bottles, perfect for soliciting research donations. Soon checks started rolling in at Caltech—twenty dollars here, fifty dollars there, sometimes $100 or even $500. The grand total only amounted to about $10,000—a far cry from the project's $342,000 budget—but Clemmons managed to secure enough additional funds to cover the materials cost for phase one of the kite-obelisk experiments... enough to construct a system of kites, pulleys, a flat sled for the obelisk to rest atop while scooting into an upright position, and a scaffold tower to demonstrate whether they were capable of lifting a two-ton obelisk.

Clemmons's effort also inspired Gharib to donate his research time. "The funding in terms of personnel came from our work-study program and my free time," says Gharib, who downplays his crucial decision. "What really made this happen was Maureen's fundraising—and not just from the cologne. She never stopped encouraging people to help the project by sending a check, and when we put it all together there was enough to get going."

The immediate goals were three-fold: to construct a scaffold tower with the required pulley system and sled, arrange for creation of a two-ton obelisk, then locate and secure permits for a test site. The first test would merely serve as a feasibility study to test the system's design, meaning there was no need to incorporate materials native to ancient Egypt. The goal was merely to demonstrate whether or not the concept would work with a heavy obelisk. "You start with less expensive materials to see if it'll work, because if it doesn't work with modern materials it sure isn't going to work with ancient materials," Gharib says. "So we purposely made that choice not to use materials from Egyptian culture, because that adds extra difficulties and it's much more expensive. Before we spent too much money, we wanted to do some tests, to make sure we had a system that worked."

That meant they could use a nylon parafoil kite rather than a linen sail, aluminum ball bearings for the pulleys, steel and composite materials to construct the tower and the sled, and contemporary synthetic ropes (rather than hemp) to link the kites with the obelisk. The system's layout was simple: the two-ton obelisk would start out prone, it's tip extending outward from the tower and the bottom edge of its base situated atop the sliding metal sled. The 425-sq.-ft. parafoil would then launch at an angle from the same side of the tower, with at least two people holding kite control lines. The primary line funneled from the obelisk, through a braking system—small, locking bearings stationed on the ground and designed to clamp down on the kite line so the obelisk would not dip back down with every wind gust—then on through the pulleys and over to the human controllers.

Graff, under Gharib's direction and the auspices of a Caltech work-study program, began the project by designing plans for the scaffold tower that would serve as a control mechanism, so they could ensure that no matter which way their kite flew the obelisk would be pulled up at a ninety degree angle. Maintaining such an angle meant they would not waste any of the wind's force, allowing the A-frame structure to guide the stone up, into place.

Fortune fell their way when news articles outlining their plan attracted the attention of Daniel Correa, president of the San Diego-based company Incablocks. Correa was accustomed to overseeing production of large concrete building materials—his company not only manufactures cement freeway barriers, it also produces interlocking blocks akin to concrete Legos that can be used to construct modular office buildings. When he read about Clemmons and the pending Caltech project in Time, Correa was intrigued. "At the time I was in the middle of building a track for the San Diego Grand Prix, using about two thousand concrete barriers that weighed six tons each," says Correa. "So when I saw them talking about lifting obelisks, I figured I was already lifting two thousand of those for the race."

Correa met with Clemmons and Gharib and offered to produce a two-ton, seventeen-foot-tall concrete obelisk for the first field test. He also offered to construct the scaffold tower, make transportation arrangements, and reserve a windy Incablocks property near a sand mine in Tecate, Mexico, as an initial test site. In effect, Correa single-handedly supplied know-how, materials, skilled volunteers, and a location—all when they were needed most. The only thing left on the project's to-do list was obtaining a much bigger kite than anything Clemmons had used in her personal field tests. She took to the Internet and found a shop in Florida that marketed a fifteen-foot wide, 425-sq.-ft. parafoil. When it arrived a few weeks later, the three of them spread the massive red and white kite across the Caltech commons, attracting a horde of engineering students.

On the weekend of October 14, 2000, Gharib, Correa, Graff and Clemmons met at the Tecate test site, helped Correa's crew construct the support tower, and waited for some wind. There wasn't any. As they watched the sun begin to set on that Sunday night, realizing they now faced a five-hour drive back to Los Angeles with no results, Gharib decided to try an alternative test. "Forget about the kite," he said. "Let's test the tower and the pulley system by hooking the obelisk to the back of a pickup truck."

Soon the rope went from the obelisk, through the pulleys and out the top of the tower just like it would have it we were using the kite. The only difference was that the truck, rather than the kite, was going to provide the force—and for the purpose of testing Graff's design for the tower and the pulleys, that was all that mattered. Clemmons held her breath as a volunteer from Correa's crew revved up the truck, put it in drive, and inched forward. The rope went taut, and the obelisk started angling upwards, as expected. It rose... and rose... and in a matter of seconds it was at an eighty-five-degree angle, nearly all the way up.

Then they heard a snap, and a clank. The obelisk crashed down, hit the desert floor, and broke in half. "Right then," Correa said later, "I decided that was the last obelisk I was going to build without using rebar for structural support."

The pulleys broke as well, as did one of the crossbars that served as a mounting bracket for the pulleys. In engineering parlance, the culprit was "a pulley-crossbar failure"—which ironically meant the field test was a success. By using a truck to evaluate the tower and pulley system, Gharib now knew they needed to alter the type of pulleys and crossbars used in the original design. "Not great results," Gharib said later, "but the testing helped us learn to work together and we found that the bar on top of the tower was not designed properly. We also found the friction on the rope and pulleys was too high, so as a result that portion of the bar broke. When we got back, I sent Emilio back to the drawing board to redesign the whole thing."

He had Correa redesign the obelisk as well, requesting a much bigger model. In early 2001, Incablocks finished an obelisk that weighed a stunning 3.4 tons. "We were aiming for three tons; the weight of the rebar added more," Correa says. "But I didn't want to build it without the rebar. I didn't want another obelisk to crack in half if we dropped it." Correa loaded the obelisk on a truck in Tecate and proceeded to try to bring it across the US border, but immigration and customs officials wouldn't let him because they thought he had something (or someone) sealed inside. "They had us there for two or three hours, and they put the whole obelisk through an X-ray machine to see that we weren't smuggling drugs or people," Correa says. "I told the customs people the whole story of building the obelisk and having to haul it up and they were laughing, they thought the whole thing was funny. It took awhile, but they finally let us go though."

Since the Tecate test indicated the project was going to require a process of trial-and-error, Gharib decided they needed a more convenient test site. "Tecate was a four-hour drive," he says, "so I couldn't imagine I'd go there every week." Efforts to use a site at California's Guadalupe Dunes became a months-long, regulatory nightmare. Then Clemmons met with Emil Theodory, a friend of Correa's who owned forty barren, windblown acres near the Mojave desert city of Quartz Hill, just outside of Palmdale, Calif.—less than a two-hour drive from Los Angeles. Theodory was excited about the project and agreed to let Caltech use his land for the experiment.

Within a few days Gharib made plans to conduct two "dry run" tests: one in April, 2001, and one in May, both using the parafoil instead of the truck. If those two were successful, Gharib would invite the public—and the news media—to attend a formal demonstration of the kite-pulley system in June, in hopes of attracting funds for additional research. It was a subtle nod to what Clemmons had learned from her first test in the park: always test the concept in private before unveiling it to the public.

Clemmons listened when Gharib told her the plan, but it took a few seconds for the significance to register. Her years-long effort was on the verge of fruition: Caltech was only one month away from using kite-power to lift a 3 ½-ton obelisk.

CHAPTER EIGHT

Kites Over The Desert

I don't usually reflect on the significance of the things I accomplish—if you stop and look at where you are, you'll fall behind everyone else, right? The project was never about me anyway. It was about the idea, and getting it out there into the world so other people could see it, consider it, and maybe even work with it. How could I have taken time out to cheer about what I'd done when the idea was still struggling for its life?

But there was one brief moment when the swell of emotion over how far things had progressed finally hit me. It didn't happen after one of the field tests, when you'd expect it. No, it actually kind of caught me by surprise in April, right before *the first test with the fifteen-foot kite. I was standing on Emil Theodory's land with my children, watching half of Quartz Hill's residents out there working to clean up the tumbleweeds and set up the equipment, and that's when it occurred to me: I had done it. Against some pretty high odds, and with the help of more people than I could count, I had somehow managed to take my backyard brainstorm and get it to the point where a major university, an entire town, and the news media were all anxious to see the results.*

It was just one brief moment, one instant in time where I gave myself a little mental pat on the back... and then it was gone. Wiped clean from a flash of worry: what if the new kite-pulley system didn't work?

That same nagging concern was on everyone's mind, for different reasons. For Gharib and Graff, it was a matter of scientific curiosity; setbacks like the one in Tecate were a natural part of the scientific process, but they were eager to demonstrate that their new design was strong enough to support the force required to lift the obelisk. Graff, working in concert with Correa and the structural engineering staff at Inca Blocks, increased the size of the pulleys and strengthened the system that held them. They also fashioned a stronger "rope brake": a locking system designed to keep the kite line from pulling backwards from the weight of the obelisk. "They improved the whole system," Gharib said. "It was a very good design, we tested it using a computer design system and I think that really helped."

For Clemmons, the pending field tests were more an issue of a search for closure. It had been a long, uphill battle, and she was eager for a chance to spread the word that her kite theory could finally be validated in conjunction with an immense object. She had visualized kites lifting massive stones and obelisks since the day the concept came to her in her backyard. Now she was hoping everyone would get a chance to see it for themselves.

In late March, Clemmons and her children joined Quartz Hill city officials and community members in digging post holes and assembling the tower. Clemmons was awed by the extent to which local residents were willing to help, particularly Fred Hartman, owner of an equipment rental shop just half-a-mile from the new test site. Hartman had already arranged for someone to retrieve the obelisk from Guadalupe Dunes to Quartz Hill, and now he was welding scaffold materials and using his rental equipment to level a section of the land.

Graff hoped to conduct a preliminary system test as soon as construction was finished, but there was no wind the entire weekend so they did the next best thing: they used a pickup truck, just like in Tecate. This time, the pulleys and the tower held the weight of the scaffolding, and within a few seconds the obelisk was standing erect.

Eager to try it with the kites, they gathered again a month later and encountered a familiar problem: no wind. Frustration rose the next morning, when the team again showed up but the wind did not. At mid-day, amid hot sun and talk of calling it quits, everyone felt something brush against their cheeks and looked around, in unison. The parafoil, secured to the ground, was bobbing, and Clemmons's anemometer was showing a steady, 12 to 18 mph breeze.

No one cheered, or made much comment. After so much time, effort, and warm weather, the group wasn't cognizant of the drama, they just got up and started hustling to their positions, knowing it might be their only opportunity to get the job done. Gharib and Graff went straight to the scaffolding, double-checking everything.

Clemmons stayed with the kite while everyone else formed an inadvertent circle around the test area. A few beats later they all looked at each other, agreed they were ready, and let the kite catch the wind.

The parafoil puffed into a comma and rose skyward, all in one smooth, easy motion. As it soared into the distance the bridle lines drew taut, and Clemmons could hear the sound of rotating wheels as the rope began sliding through the pulleys. The nose of the 3 ½-ton obelisk rose off the ground, angling upwards without hesitation as it reached forty-five degrees... seventy-five degrees... and then a full ninety degrees. It didn't stop there. Slowly, over the course of an hour-long, stop-and-go process carefully executed under Gharib's direction, the parafoil lifted the obelisk off the ground, hoisting it a full three feet into the air before a knot in the rope reached the pulleys, halting the motion. The obelisk hung from the tower, swaying pendulum-like in the breeze.

Clemmons knew the parafoil could have performed the job in just a few seconds, but that wasn't what Gharib wanted or needed in this particular experiment. Careful science demands fits and starts, meaning the group would launch the kite, let it raise the obelisk a few degrees, then stop it for discussions on how the system was performing and what their options were if the kite reacted in different ways. Science aside, they proceeded in the slow, trial-and-error fashion necessary when dealing with 3 ½-ton obelisk that could kill someone if they lost control. Clemmons kept moving her head up and then down as they proceeded, shifting her attention from obelisk to kite and then back again, too close to see both of them at once yet determined to see it all. After so much work, she couldn't bear missing any little detail.

Later that afternoon, the group lowered the obelisk back to the ground, tired and sweaty. Gharib decided some follow-up study of the redesigned pulley support bracket was in order, so they agreed to meet again in one month and left the obelisk standing upright, secured to the tower frame using rope and the pulleys to safeguard against anyone accidentally toppling it upon themselves. For Clemmons, the drive home with her kids seemed more special than the actual experiment. There was no whooping it up, or any overt celebration. Instead they had a sense of satisfaction, and several sighs of relief. One word kept forming over and over in Clemmons's head: "finally."

One month later, Clemmons and her children drove to Quartz Hill a day in advance of the next scheduled test, to check in with city officials. As her car bounced along the pothole-strewn dirt road leading to the test site, she noticed something dreadfully wrong: the obelisk was on its side. Clemmons threw open the car door, raced to the tower, and saw what had happened: vandals had stolen the pulleys from the tower, apparently cutting the rope that secured the obelisk in the process. Worse, in taking the pulleys they also took the steel support bracket that held them—the very bracket that had failed and then been redesigned after the Tecate field test, and thus needed additional testing. Clemmons, who doesn't panic easily, suddenly realized they now had no way to conduct the next morning's field test.

She phoned Graff, pulling him from his class at Caltech to see whether he had more pulleys. He did—but with the bracket missing there was no way to mount them, so he headed for the Caltech engineering shop to see if they could make another. They could... in two to three weeks. Clemmons hung up cursing, knowing she had a small army of volunteers on their way for nothing, and frustrated that they were only missing one bracket and that the engineering shop would not help even though it was only mid-day.

Frantic, she went to Hartman, who phoned a local welding company with the design for the support bracket. An hour later, the job was done, and for only $100 bucks. Problem solved... and again solved by the people of Quartz Hill, Clemmons realized. The community had come through in the clutch for her on several occasions, to the point where volunteers had even gone out to the field test site and cleaned up trash illegally dumped in the desert. The little town, she realized, had become as much a part of the engineering effort as the engineers themselves.

At that point, the only obstacle left was Mother Nature... and sure enough, when everyone arrived the next morning there was no wind. Plenty of sun, heat, and people sweating in the middle of the desert... but no wind. Noon rolled around, but the desert air remained still and the volunteers began leaving. Even Gharib got bored, so he decided to drive into town to bring back some sodas. Naturally, a short time after Gharib left the wind started picking up. In a matter of minutes, conditions were perfect: breezes at 15 mph, nice and steady.

Everyone sat there, wondering what to do with Gharib gone, knowing there was a good chance the perfect wind conditions would not last until he got back.

It wasn't much of a dilemma. After all the time everyone had been sitting around, waiting, the group decided they weren't about to wait any longer. They ran to their stations, rigged the kites... and a mere forty-five seconds later, the obelisk was raised upright. Clemmons grinned. The procedure was fast, easy, and elegant, just as she had always imagined.

Gharib came driving up the dirt road a few minutes later, seeing the obelisk swinging from the tower and the group jumping up and down with joy. He got out of the car and everyone ran up, telling him how quickly they had finished the task. Gharib laughed at his bad timing but couldn't hide his disappointment at having missed the event, and told the group to get ready for a repeat experiment. But by then the wind had picked up to 20 mph, and the engineering calculations suggested optimum wind conditions ranged from 13 mph and 19 mph. Anything more meant it was too dangerous to fly the kite. Gharib knew he would have to settle for the video instead. But he also knew that after two successful field tests they were ready for a public demonstration, ready to invite the news media and show the world that wind engineering was a feasible concept.

On June 23, 2001, that's exactly what they did. A crowd of nearly fifty visitors gathered around the scaffold tower, including reporters from *Time*, ABC News, the *Los Angeles Times*, the Associated Press, and a film crew sent by Emmy-nominated filmmaker Beth Murphy, who was gathering footage for a History Channel documentary. Clemmons joined Gharib, Graff, and Correa at their usual field test positions near the base of the tower. Already it had been a long morning. The project members, along with many of their friends and family, had been at the site since 7:30 a.m., setting up makeshift canopies for shade and grilling hot dogs to distribute to guests. Quartz Hill community members mowed the desert grasses, which were still green from spring rains, and picked up any remaining trash.

By noon the winds were gusting at speeds averaging 12 mph, the desert air was unseasonably cool, and the sky was a clear blue. Photographers encircled Clemmons as if she were a celebrity, snapping shots by the dozens every time she hugged a friend or gestured towards the kite.

Gharib and Graff were similarly swarmed. "Caltech doesn't get this much press when somebody wins a Nobel Prize," Gharib joked. Loering Johnson, who had traveled all the way from Connecticut to see his daughter's big day, regaled reporters with stories about her childhood experiments.

Just after one o'clock, Gharib and Clemmons consulted one another. Wind conditions were as perfect as they were going to get. Gharib decided it was time to fly the kite. Clemmons walked to the parafoil, speechless. She felt butterflies in her stomach again, just as she had at her very first field test in the park. This time she wasn't worried about lifting the obelisk—she knew the stone would rise after seeing how easily the kite had handled the job during the previous two field tests. But she looked around at all the people attending and realized most had donated time, money, equipment, career expertise, or just moral support so that this test could happen. For four years, more than 200 people had believed in her effort and helped her get to this point. Now, at last, she had the chance to show them their efforts were paying off.

"If realizing that doesn't give you butterflies, I don't know what does," Clemmons said. "I've been intimidated at times during this project, what with fending off the doubters and convincing people I'm not just spewing ideas, all the while trying to maintain my business and raise my children. But never have I felt so overwhelmed as in that moment: a non-scientist working hand-in-hand with some of Caltech's finest aeronautics engineers, surrounded by the press, ready to demonstrate all we had accomplished. That's when I knew this project wasn't about history anymore. It was about the here and now."

She helped lift the parafoil off the desert floor, looking at it the same way she had admired the kites in her car trunk three years earlier. Her eyes followed the lines from the parafoil to the pulleys to the obelisk. She felt her clothes being buffeted by California's closest facsimile to the Thousand Winds of Egypt. Gharib looked at her, just a quick glance, but in that instant she knew he understood what a special moment this was for both of them.

Gharib gave a nod; the group released the kite. It spun, dove, then collapsed to the ground, and Clemmons grinned. By now she was accustomed to the complexities of field tests. She knew it wasn't a big deal. She knew the kite would fly.

This time Clemmons joined Gharib in giving the signal, and up soared the kite, her emotions carried to new heights right along with it. A fraction of a second later, the nose of the massive obelisk casually rose up as well. The entire lift took only twenty-five seconds of flight time, the group's new record. Clemmons heard the crowd cheering as the obelisk lifted up, and she was cheering right along with them. For the first time in more than four thousand years, humanity had remembered to invite the wind to be its ally in raising an obelisk.

Clemmons, Gharib, Graff and Correa, all grinning, felt like they had just won the World Series, with people cheering and hooting and forming a ring around them. The news media rushed forward with questions. Clemmons was thrilled for Gharib; she knew some of his engineering cohorts had given him grief about working with an amateur and hoped all the attention meant he would get a little more support. But she also knew the day was a victory for backyard science. She had shown her children an amazing extrapolation of their simple park tests with the 400-lb. obelisk. "It's a testament to the idea that backyard science really can lead to something important, and that everything we learned when we were using the little obelisk was an important foundation for working with the bigger versions," Clemmons said. "In a way, it's a justification of everything I've believed in since I was a child."

Gharib was equally overwhelmed. "That test was refreshing," he said. "Researchers do lots of routine things, but then you go out there and something happens like that, and you see that flying is still magical. I had people that design airplanes at that test, and they got so excited... it's just different. Your heart goes pounding—is it going to fly, is it not going to fly? It's ironic they land the space shuttle right next door [at Edwards Air Force Base] to where we test, and yet this was still exciting even though it wasn't the shuttle. It's really fun to all of us at Caltech—our president saw me the next day and he joked, 'Can you lift up my library, I really want to get rid of it.' Even the people involved in Mars Lander and so many of the high tech projects have been supportive, because it's such a simple thing but a different concept. It's easy, but really imaginative, and that's why it was so refreshing."

The next morning, feature stories about the field test hit newspapers and the AP wire. ABC News aired a story that night, and soon Clemmons was talking with Fox News, the Discovery Channel, and BBC Radio, among others. Caltech ran a story and photos of the event on its website, and the usual number of site hits doubled—a reaction so unusual the site's operators left the story in a prominent position on the university's home page for more than two weeks.

Reluctant to alienate Egyptologists, Gharib made it clear in the media reports that his only interest was to demonstrate wind engineering, not pyramid construction. Nonetheless, with so many lingering questions pertaining to the Egyptian pyramids he felt obligated to investigate the archaeological issues from an engineering standpoint. That meant reverse engineering: conducting the same field test using materials that would have been available to the Egyptians. The steel scaffold and the aluminum pulleys would be replaced with wooden equivalents, aided by hemp ropes and a linen kite instead of the synthetic alternatives.

This time, the project's ever-empty bank account got some unexpected assistance when the National Geographic Society's Expedition Council stepped in, pledging to fund the next phase of research. For Clemmons the news was a dream come true: her backyard science project had burgeoned into a National Geographic Expedition. The dream continued that December when Beth Murphy—the filmmaker assembling a documentary about Clemmons and her wind engineering theory for The History Channel—asked Clemmons to travel to Egypt to shoot scenes at the Giza pyramids and other ancient historical sites. For the first time, Clemmons was able to take a firsthand look at the region's obelisks, pyramid stones, and artifacts... and to fly kites in the Egyptian desert.

Back home, Gharib and Correa decided it was time for the long pass—to ditch the 3 ½-ton obelisk and instead use the new system to hoist a monstrous hunk of stone that would more closely approximate the immense objects the ancient Egyptians were accustomed to lifting.

*Volunteers, including Clemmons's daughter Elizabeth, front
left, and son Sean, front right, assemble rebar for a 16-ton obelisk.*

They considered using granite, like ancient cultures,
but not for long; manufacturing a granite obelisk cost far
too much money and added little, if anything, to the science. So they returned to rebar-supported concrete. In
early June, 2002, Clemmons and her children joined Correa, his crew, and a group of volunteers for a long day of
construction work at the Quartz Hills field test site. Mark
Cripe, a Los Angeles County Sheriff with an extensive
background in construction, took the inexperienced volunteers under his wing when Clemmons discovered that
the cement truck hauling their anticipated load of pre-

mixed cement was already on-site—long before the obelisk's framework was ready.

The megalith's completed framework.

Clemmons and Cripe convinced the cement truck operators to wait an unprecedented three hours, repeatedly
watering their churning "mud" to keep it moist as Cripe
led the team in completing the rebar framework. For
several hours the only thing on Clemmons's mind was
"rebar, tie, rebar, tie, move-move-move, rebar, tie."

Finally, just as the cement was on the verge of hardening and the driver was ready to dump it onto the desert floor, the group finished the frame. Exhausted, Clemmons watched as the biggest concrete-pour she had ever seen oozed from the churning cement truck's gutter.

At 4:30 that afternoon, they had their result: a sixteen-ton, twenty-five-foot-tall megalith... and an appointment with the one of the most ambitious obelisk lifts in modern history.

CHAPTER NINE

Giants In The Sky

I stepped back, and a look of horror must have crossed my face. I mean, it's one thing to discuss an sixteen-ton obelisk on paper, but when you've just spent the entire day building one and you know how heavy all the materials are, you get a feel for exactly what it is you're trying to do. Let me tell you, just trying to lift ONE piece of rebar was hard, and this thing was CAKED in rebar and then filled with tons of concrete.

I stood there looking at this sixteen-ton... thing... and I started to wonder what I'd gotten these people into. Yeah, I knew that mathematically everything was supposed to work. But suddenly I was thinking, "how in God's name are we going to lift this with a KITE?" I mean, it sounds great on paper, but *when you go look that obelisk in the face... my God, that thing was huge."*

So huge, in fact, that the first lift attempt underscored the danger of what they were trying to accomplish. With winds gusting, the parafoil swept up, down, and across the test grounds in wide swaths, out of control. Clemmons watched, terrified, as a nagging fear from the very first park experiment became reality. The parafoil dipped, then swung over the landscape with tremendous speed and force—cutting right into the legs of a volunteer. The line flipped the man up and over, onto his face, before anyone could react. He spent the afternoon visiting a doctor; Clemmons and Gharib spent it reconsidering their plan.

In May, 2003, they returned to Quartz Hill with a revised kite launch system and Mark Cripe joining Daniel Correa as their unofficial construction foremen. Rather than using humans to fly the parafoil, they attached the kite's lines to four wood posts—halved telephone poles—that were embedded into the ground a few yards from the support tower. Clemmons's idea, germinated while

*Gharib and Clemmons discuss their plans as volunteers
position the sixteen-ton obelisk beneath the support tower.*

studying the pillar-like "djed columns" in ancient hieroglyphs, was simple but effective: humans would hold the
kite high enough to catch wind, then stand safely away
from the entire flight zone. The posts, rather than the
humans, would stabilize the kite. In essence, the new
posts made the system self-launching, self-stabilizing,
and much safer. Most of the overall system had also been
reverse-engineered, meaning the pulleys and the steel
sled beneath the obelisk were now made from wood, and
the A-frame scaffold tower was constructed out of pine
telephone poles (a rough approximation of the cedar
posts that the Egyptians would probably have used).

Clemmons even had a huge linen kite, custom-
manufactured in the Los Angeles garment district, ready

159

as a backup to the nylon parafoil. Everything was lab-tested, strength-tested, and wind-tunnel tested. The new system, at least on paper, was ready.

Still, the next few lift attempts brought failure and frustration. Ropes split; there was too much wind at the test site; a pulley gave way just as the obelisk was rising, sending the massive stone crashing back to the ground. For the umpteenth time, the project was stuck in a holding pattern.

Fed up and eager to accomplish something new while awaiting the next field test, Clemmons conducted her own separate experiment in late 2003, teaming with Cripe in an attempt to build a very modest, three-stone, cinder block pyramid. First they used the wind-propelled parafoil to transport each of the two-ton blocks across the top of log rollers, a plan which worked without a hitch. Then, utilizing a small A-frame structure constructed around the two side-by-side base blocks, they used the kite to slide the third block up an inclined ramp, onto the other two base stones.

"That's when moving two-ton stones became kind of normal," Cripe said. "When you first start, you're thinking 'how the hell are we going to move a two-ton stone?'

But we got quite accustomed to the weight and moving it around." For Clemmons, it was the pyramid-building equivalent of her initial family obelisk tests. It also reminded her how much she wanted to return to experimenting with her simple, core concept: kites and stones.

By January, 2004, nearly three years had passed since the team's last successful public demonstration and the group was growing haggard. While no one said they had reached their last try, Clemmons felt the unspoken understanding that something positive needed to happen or the effort might crumble. Thus far their only hint of success had come the previous autumn, when they managed to hoist the obelisk nearly forty degrees—about ten feet off the ground—before a pulley snapped. Now they were back with larger pulleys, again made of wood rather than steel. The new pulleys weren't designed to handle the wide diameter of a hemp rope, necessitating the modern-day nylon rope, but that didn't concern Gharib since Caltech's lab tests had already indicated the hemp version was more than strong enough to handle a sixteen-ton load.

Aside from Beth Murphy's documentary cameras there was no media and no large assembly of friends or colleagues, just a handful of team members and a few Quartz Hill volunteers. Regardless of the results, Clemmons realized, this was going to end much like it had begun: with a few people teaming up in a remote location, just trying to see what they could accomplish.

The moment the wind hit 22 mph, they set the parafoil free. The kite soared up, danced a bit, but remained steady. The obelisk didn't move.

No one panicked, but no one was particularly happy about it either. Clemmons reminded everyone that in the experiment when they had lifted the obelisk up forty degrees, the sled didn't start to move until the wind speed increased to 24 mph.

They waited. No movement.

A few more minutes passed. Still no movement.

Then the wind hit 24 mph on Clemmons's anemometer... and the sled scooted, just a bit. Soon, it scooted some more and the obelisk visibly angled up, toward the support tower. "Just like last time," Clemmons said. "It's like the magic happens at twenty-four or twenty-five miles per hour."

Less than a half-hour later the obelisk was ten feet off the ground—the same height it had reached when the smaller pulleys broke a few months earlier. "Look at it go!" Clemmons shouted. Even Gharib broke from his dispassionate scientist role with a big smile. "It's amazing to see this go, little by little," he said.

They heard creaks. Something cracked, loudly. Everyone stood back, waiting for the obelisk to crash down as it had the previous autumn. They scrutinized the pulleys and the support tower from afar, trying to spot the weak point. No one saw anything... and the obelisk continued rising, sliding, stopping, then rising some more, little by little.

After fifty-seven minutes, the obelisk's nose had reached the top of the tower—just beneath the pulleys, which were now too large for the stone to reach a full ninety-degree lift, but as high as it could go at about eighty-five degrees. The obelisk's base, atop the sliding ramp, sat directly underneath the tower. Clemmons let out a whoop. "We did it!" she shouted. "We did it!" Everyone broke into smiles, their happiness borne as much from relief as actual celebration. A handful of humans had erected an obelisk weighing more than sixteen tons—32,000 lbs.—using wind, wood, and ropes. The concept of using wind as a construction tool for lifting massive objects was not only mathematically possible, it was now a demonstrated, documented theory. "It didn't prove the Egyptians did it," Gharib said, "but it proved they could have done it this way, and that's the most important part."

It also proved, at least for Gharib, that there should be a place for amateurs in the research hierarchy. "Amateur scientists don't see all the complexities, so in that sense their ideas are much nicer," he said. "Maureen imagined this simple, different concept that's easy but really imaginative, and she challenged us... and so we've come up with a means of doing it. That may be why everyone at Caltech has been so supportive. Most of the time scientists are sequencing DNA, so the minute you hear about a simple idea that works there's just so much excitement."

Mark Cripe, who balanced the academic problem-solving effort with the practical know-how to construct the tower and prepare the test site, felt the effort represented science at its most fundamental level. "It's a classic example of succeeding through a series of failures," said Cripe, who gave tractor rides to researchers who could explain the physics of the vehicle's hydraulic cylinders but had never actually ridden on a tractor. "There were a lot of weekends where we would blow kite lines or rip something up and not have any forward success, then we'd go back to the drawing board. It feels good being a part of something that a lot of people thought was impossible to do."

That spring, everyone associated with the project—Clemmons, the scientists, the volunteers, the financial sponsors, family members, and Quartz Hills residents—had a chance to celebrate their achievement together at an advance screening of *Flying Pyramids, Soaring Stones,* Beth Murphy's documentary for The History Channel. The entire group, more than 250 people, toasted each other at dinner, cheered wildly when the interior lights dimmed, cheered again as they watched the documentary, and yet again when the lights returned. There were no Egyptologists in the crowd... and no one cared. The science was a success, the wind engineering theory was on the verge of being presented both nationally and internationally, and all the hard work had paid off.

Clemmons knew the sixteen-ton obelisk lift was probably her final collaboration with Gharib. The aeronautics engineer had other research obligations, and couldn't volunteer his time forever. And Clemmons, inspired by the three-stone mini-pyramid she had built the previous winter, had other plans. After addressing the crowd at the screening, the two collaborators parted with a tender hug. Maybe it was the thrill of the achievement, or the sight of the amateur and the professional celebrating their success, but that simple hug between Clemmons and Gharib drew applause.

Of course, the crowd assumed that with the sixteen-ton obelisk lifted and The History Channel documentary on the air, the project had reached an end. Clemmons knew otherwise. "I want to get back to kites and stones, the way I envisioned it," she said. "No pulleys, no towers, nothing fancy. Just kites and stones."

Lifting obelisks was one thing, she figured, but it didn't necessarily offer a direct connection to the pyramids. What she had wanted to do all along, from that first blustery, backyard moment when she envisioned the kite theory, was demonstrate that a kite could heft the dead weight of a two-ton stone up the side of a looming pyramid. That meant she needed to assemble a modest, incomplete pyramid using modern methods, hook a kite to an immense stone, and see whether wind and kite—in concert with some simple form of ramp or roller true to the technology of ancient Egypt—were enough to lift that stone atop one of the pyramid walls.

Fortune smiled when Dave Culp, who set a world record for constructing the largest kite to pull a boat, read Internet reports about Clemmons and decided to offer assistance. "My company developed a proprietary kite as a replacement for spinnaker sails on racing yachts," Culp said, "and it occurred to me that this was technology that might have been available to the ancients, because the engineering doesn't rely on modern aerodynamics and it can be built with ancient materials." Culp's kite, a "minimal-energy spheroid surface," maintains tension on every square inch of the cloth, meaning the kite always provides maximum lift. Clemmons liked the design simplicity of its half-balloon shape, since there is no evidence that the ancient Egyptians had the aerodynamic knowledge necessary for parafoils. Intrigued, she commissioned Culp to build a six-foot-by-eight-foot version made of silk, rather than linen, due to cost considerations.

Field tests ensued as Clemmons, Cripe and Culp used the new kite to tug stones across the ground and lift them, all in hopes of eventually hoisting one atop a small pyramid. Always, they ran into the same obstacle.

"It took us three years of ramp-stress to figure out that the simplest ramp is the best: just use the pyramid as the ramp," Clemmons said. "After all the stuff we've been through you would think that any moron could see that, but you can't believe what we went through looking at ramps. I mean, we studied dirt ramps, wooden ramps, what to use for rollers... all of it, over and over. But it turns out one or two log rollers, that's all you need. So it was like, okay, we'll throw a couple of log rollers in, then just use the natural ramp of the pyramid to move the stone up to the top."

She mentioned her plan during a 2007 presentation to the American Institute of Architects and, after receiving two standing ovations, received something even more uplifting the following day: an offer from California State Polytechnic University in Pomona, Calif., to help her assemble the pyramid she had in mind. The following year, a hundred of the university's architecture students designed the pyramid stones, cast them, and helped haul them to the same desert test site where Clemmons had lifted the obelisks.

Culp hauled something as well: a monster kite measuring thirty-five feet tall and sixty feet wide while aloft, and more than one hundred feet wide and fifty-five feet tall when grounded. "We needed a kite that could pull something a short distance with lots of power—so basically, pick the block up and smack it back down again," Culp said. "One of the things my company patented was the fundamental engineering behind a kite which allowed us to build it very large without building it heavy, and without modern materials."

Cal Poly had initially hoped to have the students spend two weeks assisting Clemmons with field tests; schedules and other complications limited them to just three days. After two days of soil-preparation and moving the stones into place using muscle and tools depicted in Egyptian art, they had a grand beginning: a 14-foot-tall, 53-stone, 200-ton pyramid... or at least, the first seven rows of a pyramid, more than enough to serve as a ramp for the flight test.

But the two-day effort left just one day to complete the job. Clemmons knew from experience that everything would have to go perfectly for her brand new kite to pull a two-ton stone up the side of the pyramid that day. She also knew that rarely had anything gone perfectly in her ten years of field tests. This time was no exception: the wind wasn't very strong and then, while testing flight conditions, the kite snagged on a clump of sage brush, tearing it. "The kite was a disaster," she said. "I felt really bad because it was the last day and we were supposed to be flying the stone, but the kite and the wind were just not cooperating and that was it."

The assembled group, thirty students and ten volunteers, went home dejected. The semester was over. The class was finished. The project, albeit incomplete, was done.

Clemmons, of course, was not. "You always need to finish things," she knew. "I needed to show Cal Poly the effort was worth it. No loose ends." So, she had Culp produce another kite. She called Mark Cripe for his field expertise. She rounded up friends and cobbled things together, same as always.

On August 3, 2008, she, Cripe and Culp were in the desert with volunteers once again, prepping the kite, checking the anemometer. Only the wind was missing... until afternoon, when the breeze finally rose to a near-perfect nine miles per hour.

"You know... if this doesn't work, you'll know your theory doesn't work," Cripe told her.

Clemmons, thinking it over, realized he was right.

"I have the kite I want, made of natural material," she said. "I have my pyramid. I have my stone. I have my log roller, and the wind is coming up. All the stars and planets are now aligned. Meaning, if this doesn't work..."

She didn't see a need to finish the thought. Instead she looked at the kite and the stone, admiring the simplicity, knowing it was a dead pull. After one last check of the wind, she shouted the words everyone was waiting for.

"Do it!" she said.

The kite launched, rising straight up as always. Clemmons expected a momentary pause in the action when the rope pulled taut, but there was no pause whatsoever. As soon as the rope straightened the two-ton stone block moved... and moved fast, as if a giant was pulling a sled. The block slid up the side of the pyramid, leaped on top, then continued, soaring off the other side until it came to a stop a full twelve feet from the pyramid's base.

The entire process took just four seconds.

Everyone whooped and hollered... then raced to pull the release cords, fearing the kite might drag the stone into some downfield power lines. As the group downed the kite, Clemmons didn't say anything. She simply fell to her knees.

"Thanks, God," she said softly. "This works. This really works."

She now refers to the moment that the two-ton stone went up and over the pyramid as "my 'Wright Brothers moment.' Do we have to improve the control system? Yeah. Just like the Wright Brothers: once you get the thing in the air and you see it's working, then you see if you can fix this, fix that, whatever. It's the same model. Once that stone went up and over... hey, already we've got five different control systems that we want to try. But all of that's just a matter of improving the control. Once that stone went up I knew for sure, yeah, this works. That was the watershed moment."

Appropriately, once the kite line was severed Clemmons brought out a surprise: champagne, on ice. Together she and her friends popped it open and hoisted a toast—not to kites, or Egyptians, but to the power of simplicity.

"The simplest solutions are the best: just harness the wind," Clemmons says. "There's nobody pushing or pulling the stone. There's nobody flying the kite. This was about getting back to kites and stones. We just hooked them up and let them go. People say you have to have control systems, but no, you have to work into that. The first question is, given free reign, can the kite pull the stone up? We now know the answer: it can."

She also knows something else. She knows, given the simplicity of the experiment, that there is no reason the ancient Egyptians couldn't have done the exact same thing.

CHAPTER TEN

The Future Of
The Past

I guess there are people out there who figured that since I wasn't an engineer they could dismiss the whole kite engineering theory—as if you have to have a degree to do science. Well, you don't. Anyone can do science. You just have to do the same thing Alexander Graham Bell did—you research your topic as much as you can, you go out in the field with your family or anyone who's willing to help, and you test the idea. That's what science—true science—is all about. It's not about getting a degree, or publishing papers in journals. It's about falling in love with the idea and the "feel" of experimenting, and cultivating that love for science with your kids. It's *also about getting out there and trying something new... and if that means starting in your backyard, then why not?*

I'll keep field testing this kite theory and then, after I've fully demonstrated the feasibility, I'll just step back and let smarter minds than mine take that idea, run with it, and make it better than anything I could ever possibly have done. That's all I've ever wanted since I started: for better minds than mine to consider this seriously, to study it, and to say, "here's a viable tool." And you know what? Maybe when they work out the details some of this project's ideas will be proven wrong— the shape of the kite, my interpretation of the tools, or whatever. That's fine—the important thing is that people will not only understand that the Egyptians might have used the wind, they'll also realize how useful the wind can be today.

That realization has slowly, steadily begun. *Construction and Culture: A Built Environment*, an engineering textbook written by Donald E. Mulligan and Kraig Knutson of Arizona State University's Del E. Webb School of Construction, now cites Clemmons's wind theory as a possible construction method. The Explorers Club, an international society for advancing scientific field research, was so impressed with her work that they granted her membership as a fellow—a level reserved for individuals who have made documented contributions to scientific knowledge. WINGS WorldQuest, an organization celebrating women who advance science, bestowed the same honor and, in a fun tribute, included her on a card deck depicting female explorers. Universities and professional societies regularly contact Clemmons with lecture requests... as do community organizations and schools.

Despite her focus on kites as four-thousand-year-old construction tools, Clemmons is convinced that harnessing wind as a power source might prove just as useful today, at a time when fossil fuels are costly and greenhouse gas emissions are on everyone's mind. She has already received inquiries from engineers in Third-World countries who are searching for construction methods that might help them avoid obtaining caterpillars, cranes, and other multimillion-dollar pieces of equipment that use tons of fuel. "Once we finish demonstrating this technology," Clemmons says, "we can not only use it to understand ancient cultures but apply it to remote areas of the world that don't have a lot of financial resources."

Those same areas may benefit from Clemmons's corollary research. During field tests, when she needed to firm up loose soil prior to moving stones and obelisks, she found that the enzymes in beer (a beverage that the ancient Egyptians enjoyed) turned the dirt surfaces rockhard in a matter of minutes—far more quickly, and cheaply, than using heavy equipment. Clemmons is now consulting with a soil stabilization company that is incorporating easy, inexpensive methods for compacting surfaces beneath oil field roads and construction sites.

On days when her imagination roams free, Clemmons envisions kites assembling structures on other worlds. While giving a presentation to a group of aeronautic engineers and meteorologists at the NASA-Dryden Test Flight facility, she broached the idea of using kites for heavy construction on Mars. To her surprise, the crowd was very interested because Mars has frequent windstorms, there's no fossil fuel, and solar power isn't as efficient as on Earth because the sun is much further away. The wind, therefore, might offer an easy means for handling heavy construction—an option NASA researchers hope to investigate.

In the meantime, skeptics will retain the higher ground when it comes to ancient wind engineering. Clemmons vows not to let it slow her down. She doesn't understand the prevailing skepticism, or Egyptology's reluctance to investigate what she considers a sensible solution to an age-old construction enigma. That innocent charm of an intelligent woman living in her own idyllic frame of mind probably saved her project. People can sense when a cause comes not from personal gain or self-promotion, but from the heart. That's what the kite theory is to Clemmons, and the undying enthusiasm she wore on her sleeve helped her find legitimate researchers, financial sponsors, community support, and a vast amount of individual expertise. It's also how, after several years, she finally convinced this skeptical journalist that you don't need a degree in science to be one damn good scientist.

Even Caltech's Gharib, who distances himself from many of Clemmons's Egypt-related claims, credits her for what became one of the university's most notable projects in recent years. "Without her excitement and encouragement, I don't think we could have done it," he says. "Maureen was the key. She got it started and kept it going. She knows how to talk to different levels of people, from the guy that sweeps the floor to the president of the company. That's what helped us get problems solved as we went along... and that's why I would say my respect for her skills went from ten to one hundred as we moved forward."

There's a chance that Clemmons's effort was all for naught. As noted earlier, archaeologist Mark Lehner followed up on his *Nova* work in dramatic fashion, using the sand-ramp method to erect a twenty-five-ton obelisk, confirming the technique as a means for erecting obelisks and moving large stones. Perhaps in the coming years Egyptologists will ascertain a complete list of construction methods used to build the pyramids, and that list will not include kites. Perhaps they will be able to demonstrate that the prevailing theories involving levers, ramps, and rollers are indeed the entire solution; perhaps they will even be able to duplicate the feat by constructing a full-sized pyramid using ancient techniques.

But that hasn't happened so far, and considering the amount of effort necessary just to find an Egyptologist willing to consider alternative theories, it doesn't seem likely. To this day, even though there is no dispute that the ancient Egyptians were sailors and the validity of kite power has now been demonstrated by researchers from Alexander Graham Bell to Morteza Gharib, not one mainstream, university-affiliated Egyptologist has been willing to step forward and concede that there is at least a remote possibility Clemmons could be on to something.

Not one.

That, more than anything else, is the reason you find this book before you. It isn't about demanding that you change your viewpoint, and it certainly isn't meant as a condemnation of Egyptologists' good work. No one, including Clemmons, disputes the notion that levers, ramps and rollers were a part of the construction process. But having answers and having *all* the answers are two different things. Egyptologists don't have all the answers, and whether they eventually subscribe to Clemmons's kite theory or not, they will certainly need to embrace her willingness to think outside the box if the remaining answers are ever to be found.

"The challenge now, for everyone, is to see whose method can erect something on the scale of what the Egyptians were actually lifting," she says. "That's why this is only the beginning. I'll keep building miniature pyramids out of however many two-ton stones it takes, because I want people to see how easy it will be. Other research expeditions had a bunch of men pushing and pulling, sweating and grunting. Mine will be me and my girlfriends, sitting in lawn chairs with kites and a twelve-pack of beer, waiting for the wind to kick up."

Perhaps demonstrating a new pyramid construction method isn't the most significant aspect of what Clemmons has achieved. This is a woman who took an innovative idea and didn't give up on it. Criticism, rejection, severe financial hardship, numerous setbacks... none of it mattered. Instead she fervently advanced the idea from her backyard to the local park, to the Caltech campus, to the Mojave desert... all the way into the international consciousness. Most important, her children—both now adults—grew up absorbing every moment of it. Elizabeth, a Los Angeles County Science Fair winner during high school, is a graduate student studying to become a veterinarian. Sean, who became a licensed aircraft pilot at age 18, is an airport operations officer in Michigan. Years ago, he and a friend won Lockheed-Martin's Stellar Design Challenge for designing a hydrogen-filled blimp to explore Mars. His co-winning friend? Muhammad Khan... the neighbor who joined the Clemmons family on so many of their childhood experiments. The backyard science, it seems, made a difference.

Make no mistake: Clemmons's kite theory hasn't yet led to construction of a full-scale replica pyramid. But if she hasn't built a pyramid, she has climbed a mountain. Now the only thing left to see is whether any of Egyptology's gurus are willing to sacrifice their pride long enough to hear her out.

ACKNOWLEDGMENTS

From Maureen Clemmons:

This project would not have become reality without devoted help from hundreds of individuals who remain unmentioned in this book. Over the course of my work, from inception to completion, I was blessed to meet many people who share a passion for knowledge, exploration, and the excitement of testing new ideas. I apologize that this manuscript does not afford the opportunity to mention by name the many people and organizations who dedicated time, resources, encouragement and knowledge. Their efforts helped translate my ideas into reality, and pushed my field tests into the annals of history. Thank you, and God bless you all.

I would also like to acknowledge our innovative, historical giants—including Galileo Galilei, Alexander Graham Bell, Katherine Wright, and Eugene Shoemaker—for their inspiration, tenacity and insight, especially when navigating uncharted knowledge, repeated failures, deep discouragement... and finally, resounding success.

From Dan Cray:

Much love and appreciation to my wife Jane, for pointing her skeptical boyfriend (now husband) down this fascinating path.

Many thanks as well to the backyard scientists (Maureen's family and friends) who took the time to share the thrills, and challenges, of their endeavors. Also to Mory Gharib and his colleagues, for their ability to explain the complexities of aeronautics and fluid dynamics in everyday language.

If you'll pardon me for stretching back a few years, I'd like to thank Jeff Kleinman for his professionalism and determination. My sincere thanks to Lisa Lytton as well, for her concise yet enduring editorial perspective.

And of course, to Maureen Clemmons. Thanks, Maureen, for not giving up when the odds (and the Egyptologists, and the corporations) said you should… and for showing the world that endearing, creative, intelligent scientists don't always look like Doc Brown.

ABOUT THE AUTHORS

Innovation consultant Maureen Clemmons holds an EdD in Organization Change and an Executive MBA from Pepperdine University. She is president of Transformations, a consulting firm specializing in change management and innovation. WINGS WorldQuest, an organization celebrating women who advance science, and the Explorer's Club, an international society for advancing scientific field research, elected her a fellow for her pioneering achievements. Clemmons lives with her family in Reseda, California.

Dan Cray covered science and news as a *Time* journalist for twenty-three years, reporting more than sixty cover stories and sharing a National Headliner Award for coverage of the O.J. Simpson verdict. He is also a novelist and holds a degree in English from UCLA. He lives in Los Angeles with his wife and son.

Thank you for reading!

You're invited to share your thoughts and reactions
at any of your favorite book review sites.

For additional information, photos, background
material, and information about the wind engineering
project, please visit Maureen Clemmons at
www.trans4mations.com

Made in the USA
Middletown, DE
02 June 2018